GREEN LIES
And Other BS

John Mullinder

Copyright © 2021 by John Mullinder

All rights reserved.

No part of this book may be reproduced in any form or by any electronic or mechanical means, including information storage and retrieval systems, without written permission from the author, except for the use of brief quotations in a book review.

Every effort has been made to include accurate and current references in the Endnotes and Key Sources. Some of the URLs may have been changed or removed after the publication date.

ISBN: 978-0-994871-11-4

For Carol, who can smell BS a mile away.

Contents

Key Terms ... 7
Introduction ... 9
Chapter 1: "Ancient" Forests ... 14
Chapter 2: Boreal Forest ... 20
Chapter 3: Cardboard ... 24
Chapter 4: Deforestation ... 27
Chapter 5: "Degraded" Forest ... 34
Chapter 6: Environmentally Friendly, Eco-Friendly ... 37
Chapter 7: Exaggeration ... 39
Chapter 8: Forest ... 44
Chapter 9: Forest Cover ... 49
Chapter 10: Fresh Trees Are Needed Because Paper Is In Landfill ... 53
Chapter 11: Generation (Of Waste) ... 55
Chapter 12: Google ... 57
Chapter 13: Hundred (100%) Fully, Completely ... 59
Chapter 14: Hypocrisy? ... 63
Chapter 15: "Killing" And "Saving" Trees ... 66
Chapter 16: "Old-Growth" Forest ... 72
Chapter 17: Omissions ... 78
Chapter 18: Packaging Waste ... 83
Chapter 19: "Paperless" ... 87
Chapter 20: Pizza Boxes ... 89
Chapter 21: Pristine And Undisturbed Forest ... 91
Chapter 22: "Recoverable" ... 93

Chapter 23: Recovery And Recycling Rates 95
Chapter 24: Recyclable 101
Chapter 25: Recycled 106
Chapter 26: Recycled Content. 110
Chapter 27: Recycled *versus* Recyclable 114
Chapter 28: Recycling 117
Chapter 29: Responsible Sourcing (Chain-Of-Custody Certification) 120
Chapter 30: Reusable. 121
Chapter 31: Sugarcane (Bagasse). 124
Chapter 31: Sustainable. 128
Chapter 32: Toilet Paper. 130
Chapter 33: "Tree-Free". 133
Chapter 34: Waste (Definitions) 141
Chapter 35: Xmas Paper 145
Chapter 36: "Zero" Waste 149
Chapter 37: Conclusion 151
Acknowledgements 154
Key Sources 155
Appendix 1. 158
Endnotes. 163

KEY TERMS

The following words and phrases recur as fundamental terminology in many of the entries in this book.

ancient: Are we talking about civilizations, trees, or people? The oldest living trees are 5,000 years old. Most of Canada's trees are less than 100 years old. For more, see **"ANCIENT" FORESTS**.

boreal: The boreal zone is different to the North American boreal zone and the Canadian boreal zone and the Canadian boreal forest. Confused? All is explained at **BOREAL FOREST**.

circular economy: Ah, at last a definition! Although there are several on this subject. Here is Environment and Climate Change Canada's: "The circular economy is a different way of doing business. The way our economies extract, use, then dispose of resources is putting pressure on our natural systems, communities, and public health. This is a linear economy – it moves in a straight line from resource extraction to waste disposal. In a circular economy, nothing is waste. The circular economy retains and recovers as much value as possible from resources by reusing, repairing, refurbishing, remanufacturing, repurposing, or recycling products and materials. It's about using valuable resources wisely, thinking about waste as a resource instead of a cost, and finding innovative ways to better the environment and the economy."

deforestation: Not what most people think it is. The confusion over where forest cover loss and deforestation begin and end has led to a lot of sloppy journalism, false headlines, and misleading claims about deforestation that continue to this day. Check out **DEFORESTATION** and **FOREST COVER** to be confused no more!

"degraded" forest: The United Nations asked 236 countries if they were monitoring degraded forest. Although 10% didn't respond, 68% did and said no, they weren't. There are major problems with defining and measuring this term. See **"DEGRADED" FOREST.**

forest: There are 60,000 different species of tree and almost as many definitions of *forest*, it seems. However, the United Nations has broken it all down into two major categories and a couple of sub-categories. Check out the big picture at **FOREST.**

generation (of waste): The misuse of this term is one of the most frustrating media boo-boos around. And it's not entirely the media's fault! All is explained at **GENERATION (OF WASTE).**

"old-growth" forest: Take your pick as there are at least two definitions to choose from: retaining the world's primary forests whatever their age, or just looking at old trees and deciding whether they should be harvested or not. More at **"OLD-GROWTH" FOREST.**

"recoverable": Sorry, no official definition. Anything can be recovered if you throw enough money at it.

recovery and recycling rates: This is a boondoggle. We can make it whatever you want it to be. Check out **RECOVERY AND RECYCLING RATES.**

recyclable: How is it that aluminum foil can be labelled recyclable yet only 3% of it actually gets collected? Enter the world of recyclable and what's actually recycled. There's plenty to choose from here: **RECYCLED, RECYCLED versus RECYCLABLE, RECYCLING,** and **RECOVERY AND RECYCLING RATES.**

waste: It's not as if anyone is deliberately lying here. *Mostly!* It's just that many people do not speak or write as precisely as they should, or are ill-informed, or use statistics incorrectly, or tend to exaggerate depending on their specific agenda or knowledge base. Check out **WASTE (DEFINITIONS).** You'll never see waste the same way again!

INTRODUCTION

I was maybe five years old when my older brother conned me into sinking my teeth into a piece of cow turd. I'm assuming it was cow turd because the few bulls on my uncle's farm were penned separately, and visiting townies like us were warned to stay away from them or else. Not that we did, of course. I remember scrambling for the fences once with an angry bull in hot pursuit because that same smart brother of mine had heaved a rock at it. Ah, the fond memories of childhood down on the farm!

But getting back to the turd. "Sinking my teeth" into this hard bovine patty is overstating it. More like cautiously brushing it with my lips. Although that could be revisionist history on my part.

I have no idea what my wise and obviously overprotective sibling told me at the time. But it must have been really convincing. Along the lines of *"just like apple pie."* And I'm sure he blatantly lied about chomping down on one himself. Yeah, many times.

Anyway, whether bite or brush, my only memory of that day is of a dry flaky taste of pastry nothingness. Definitely not apple pie. My brother, of course, takes great delight in reminding me of this incident today, preferably when other people are around. And I freely acknowledge my gullibility. Hey, I was only five!

But maybe I learned far more from that innocent little chomp-down than one might expect: Be wary of the con man and the smooth talker. And check out the apple pie first. In my early career in journalism, I really enjoyed the digging around, the research, the peeling back of the onion to get to the facts before putting pen to paper or, today, keyboard to computer.

And in my second career, working on environmental policy issues, I discovered a wide-open field of opportunity for those inclined to mislead, obscure, exaggerate, spin, lie, and just plain old bullshit. And it's not always the sales and marketing types. It's environmental groups and governments as well. In fact, we all fudge issues and facts when it serves our purposes.

Who among us has not peddled a résumé that just slightly embellishes a few points, maybe leaves something out, or inflates the importance of a contribution? Come on, let's be honest. Some of the BS outlined here, though, is far more serious in its consequences than the small indiscretions most of us are guilty of.

That's why I wrote this book. There is a huge amount of misinformation, hyperbole, omissions, and rampant confusion about so many environmental issues today, especially on social media. Did you know that there's no such thing as an ancient forest? That cardboard doesn't exist? That nothing is 100% recyclable or compostable? That generating waste doesn't mean dumping it? That real recycling rates are just over 30%? That wheat straw is not as good as it's cracked up to be? And that sugarcane (bagasse) is not waste?

You could spend a whole lifetime correcting some of this stuff. And getting mountains of nasty and anonymous abuse for doing so. So, I guess I'm sticking my neck out here by presenting the facts as I know them. *Somebody's got to do it!*

I have assembled almost 40 unique entries, arranged alphabetically for ease of reference. And I have tried to ground-truth every single one of them with the information sources provided in the **ENDNOTES** and **KEY SOURCES** at the back of the book. I have also tried to keep the entries as concise as possible.

Many of them are inter-related. For example, there are obvious connections between the terms *recycling, recycled, recyclable,* and *recovery and recycling rates*. The same applies to the *generation of* and *diversion of waste*. Words and definitions have distinct meanings that are unfortunately often confused.

There are also commonly used words that require clarification in the context in which they usually appear. The terms *deforestation, degradation,* and *forest cover loss* are frequently bandied around as if they mean the same thing. They don't. Then there's the straight-out little green lies, the exaggerations, the significant omissions, and, yes, the sheer hypocrisy of some claimants.

I recognize that a lot more of these little (and not so little) green lies are circulating in cyberspace than I have included here. I have largely focussed on issues from the United States and Canada, although many of the topics are international in scope. Much of the data I have used is Canadian because I am more familiar with it.

The choice of entries also reflects the limits of my own personal knowledge and work experience (the paper industry, packaging, recycling, and waste issues). But that's where you come in. I welcome suggestions for further entries. And, of course, the few people who don't like what I've written *(surely not!)* can always suggest changes or updates. But just the facts please. I've had my fill of apple pie.

LITTLE GREEN LIES
And Other BS
(FROM "ANCIENT" FORESTS TO "ZERO" WASTE)

A Consumer and Media Guide

Postscript: Right on publication deadline, Competition Bureau Canada released a document titled *Environmental Claims and Greenwashing*. It acknowledges that there has been an increase in false and misleading ads or claims, also known as greenwashing, and urges businesses to avoid vague claims such as "eco-friendly" or "safe for the environment." It says consumers should be vigilant against environmental claims that seem vague, exaggerated, or that are not accompanied by supporting statements, and that they should not be afraid to reach out to manufacturers to ask them questions.

It then drops this information. "The Competition Bureau has archived *Environmental Claims: A Guide for Industry and Advertisers*. The guide may not reflect the bureau's current policies or practices and does not reflect the latest standards and evolving environmental concerns. The guide will remain available for reference, research, and recordkeeping purposes but will not be altered or updated as of the date of archiving."

Why not? In the absence of further clarification, this seems like a cop-out to me. If there are more claims and the current guide is out-of-date, then why not update it? If it's important enough to counter greenwashing, then the resources necessary to update it (our taxes) should be allocated to get the job done. Without an update or some other semi-legal guidance, we're only going to get *more* little green lies and BS, not less.

John Mullinder, November 5, 2021.

Chapter 1

"Ancient" Forests
Sorry folks, but there are none!

Branding the world's primary[1] forests as ancient is probably one of the slickest con jobs in recent environmental history. Because *ancient* forests (in the normal sense of the word) are few and far between, if they exist at all.

For a successful environmental campaign, you need a credible cause, a catchy word or phrase, to paint yourself as the hero and somebody else as the villain, and to tie it all together with a sizable dose of emotion. It helps when there's a definitional vacuum or confusion at the time of launch. In the case of forestry there certainly was, especially with the various definitions of *forest* floating around. Some preferred to label forests as original, natural, or virgin. Others favoured primeval, primary, pristine, old-growth, or even late seral.

Greenpeace opted for ancient. Back in 2006, the environmental group proclaimed the boreal forest of Canada "one of the largest tracts of *ancient* forest in the world" (emphasis added). But Greenpeace did not define ancient forests in terms of how old the trees were. "Ancient forests are forests that are shaped largely by natural events with little impact from human activities," it declared. So basically, in its view, forest minus humans equals ancient. These "ancient" forests include all large intact forest landscapes but also smaller intact forests, "from saplings to old giants."[2]

In subsequent years, a Vancouver-based conservation group called Canopy has taken the "ancient" campaign to another level, promoting the Ancient and Endangered Forests brand (capitalized to make it more impressive) and boosting an Ancient Forest Friendly logo scheme that corporations can buy into and then use to brag about their environmental credentials.

The media has got into the act as well, with journalists and bloggers slipping in the word *ancient* to describe forests or trees, with little or no consideration as to whether its use is appropriate or accurate.

Let me be very clear here: *The cause of conserving and protecting the world's remaining primary forests is commendable.* And many of these forests are certainly endangered. I don't have a problem with the cause. And I have no wish to step into the emotional cauldron of British Columbia politics and how its people handle what are commonly called old-growth forests. My objection here is to the hijacking of the meaning of the word ancient *for emotional and commercial purposes, and to the media's continued and inaccurate use of the word.*

For most people, *ancient* means "really old"

The word *'ancient'* means "old" for most people, as in *"really* old." And Canada's forests are not old. Think of the ancient civilizations of Africa and Asia, of the Incas and the Mayans, and of the ancestors of today's Indigenous peoples. Check out a dictionary or a thesaurus for the meaning of *ancient* and you will see definitions or synonyms like "very old," "having existed for a very long time," "belonging to a time that was long ago," "antique, obsolete."

What's ancient?

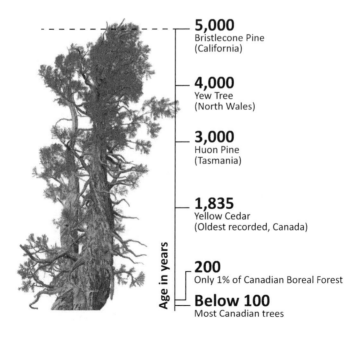

5,000
Bristlecone Pine
(California)

4,000
Yew Tree
(North Wales)

3,000
Huon Pine
(Tasmania)

1,835
Yellow Cedar
(Oldest recorded, Canada)

200
Only 1% of Canadian Boreal Forest

Below 100
Most Canadian trees

Age in years

When we look at the world's trees, the oldest living species is the bristlecone pine of the Southwestern United States at more than 5,000 years old. There's a yew tree in North Wales that's supposedly 4,000 years old; and the Huon pines of Tasmania (Australia) clock in at about 3,000 years old. In tree-age terms, these are legitimately ancient.[3]

North America's trees and forests are pimply teenagers by comparison. In Canada, for example, the eastern white cedar and the Douglas fir are both capable of topping a mere 1,000 years.[4] That sounds pretty impressive to relatively short-lived humans but in tree-age terms there's no way those trees qualify as ancient.

Canada's oldest trees grow primarily in two ecozones: the temperate rainforest of the British Columbia coast, and the Montane Cordillera which stretches from north-central British Columbia southeast to the Alberta foothills and south to the US border. But these admittedly "old" trees (mainly fir, hemlock, spruce and cedar) collectively represent only 4% of Canada's total forest population. The *great majority* of trees in Canada's forests (spruce, poplar, pine) are aged between 41 and 120 years old, with most of them (25%) in the 81-100-year range.[5]

So, from a purely age point of view, it is abundantly clear that there are no ancient forests in Canada. In fact, most Canadian trees are less than 100

Most Canadian trees are below 100 years old

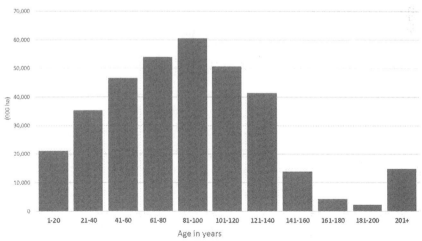

Source: *National Forest Inventory* (Canada), Table 14

years old! And if you look at the boreal alone, only 1% of its trees makes it to more than 200 years old![6] To describe them or the boreal forest as ancient, then, is BS.

Continuously changing ecological cycle

There's another reason that Canadian scientists don't like the use of the word *ancient*, especially as it applies to the boreal forest. According to Natural Resources Canada: "Scientists do not consider the boreal forest to be ancient because the forest itself is subject to ongoing natural disturbances (such as insect infestations and fire) that are part of an ecological cycle that renews the forest." [7] In other words, while the land that the forests inhabit might be ancient, the forests themselves are not. There is no such thing as an ancient forest if it is continuously changing because of climatic and other disturbances.

Ask the forest scientists of the world what they think. The Food and Agriculture Organization of the United Nations (FAO) has been debating for decades how to define and categorize the world's many different types of forest. They've come up with several definitions, and ancient isn't among them (see **FOREST**).

Canopy's own explanation of its Ancient and Endangered Forests brand doesn't help much either.[8] It cites three documents, but none of them defines *ancient*. One is titled "Endangered Forests" and goes into quite some technical detail about them, but ancient forests are neither specifically defined nor mentioned. Being endangered is quite different to being ancient. And being rare is not ancient either. Our sports champions have rare athletic abilities, but I don't think they'd be too happy to be called ancient.

Even the scientist whom Canopy quotes as being supportive doesn't use the word *ancient* in any of the published articles I have viewed, preferring *primary* forest instead.[9] Significantly, the non-profit World Resources Institute also declines to use the word *ancient*, opting for the term *old-growth*. *Old-growth* has several different meanings (see **"OLD-GROWTH" FOREST**) but in Canada it generally applies to trees more than 200 to 250 years old. Those trees are clearly not ancient.

Thus, Canopy's Ancient Forest Friendly brand is basically a *marketing and fund-raising exercise* that has little to do with the age of trees. How can you be Ancient Forest Friendly when there are no ancient forests?[10]

When challenged recently on its use of the word *ancient*, Canopy claimed that "an ancient forest is not defined by the age of the individual trees." Well, that's interesting, given how often it mentions them. Rather, Canopy said, *ancient* refers to the whole forest ecosystem. "For example, while boreal forest trees will grow up to be 80-200 years old, the forest ecosystem that has evolved there is over 8000 years old and vast swaths have never been industrially logged before. The evolved ecosystem of the boreal is older than the pyramids." [11]

So now we are talking about a whole forest eco-system that's ancient, not just a forest. An underground fungal network, for example.[12] What happens if a forest that's been in place for several hundred years is logged? Does this damage an ancient subterranean network that has developed over centuries? Does the underground network have to start from scratch? We have no idea.

But if we accept this argument, doesn't it apply to *all* trees? We shouldn't log *any* trees because all trees have this possibility of an ancient connection? Same with the sea. The sea is definitely ancient, but most of the fish that live in it are not. Should we stop harvesting fish because the seawater they live in is ancient? Canopy doesn't think so.[13]

Some people will say what does it matter whether you call the trees ancient or old-growth or something else, they're still being cut down, this is just an academic pin-pricker of a debate. An understandable viewpoint certainly, given the emotions surrounding the conservation and protection of British Columbia's remaining old-growth forests in particular. But telling the truth about Canada's forests is important too.

Canopy continues to trot out stuff like "thousand-year-old-forests are being destroyed to make boxes" when, in fact, most Canadian trees and forests are less than 100 years old. Mugging and killing a 30, 40 or 50-year-old person is bad enough. Mugging and killing a 94-year-old is infinitely worse on any social scale. *Ancient* is an emotional and fundraising multiplier. That's why it's there. It's BS.

See also **BOREAL FOREST, FOREST, "OLD-GROWTH" FOREST, and PRISTINE AND UNDISTURBED FOREST.**

Older trees attract sympathy, funding

The word *ancient* may not be used but there are other ways to attract sympathy and support. And with a pliant media that doesn't bother to fact-check, the little green lies are broadcast everywhere.

- New York based Natural Resources Defense Council talks about "centuries-old" trees hewn from the Canadian boreal, and Indigo Books and Music CEO Heather Reisman refers to "centuries-old forests" when, in fact, most of the trees in the boreal are less than 100 years old and only 1% is more than 200 years old.[14]
- Canopy claims that "thousand-year-old forests are being destroyed to make boxes" and posts a cartoon with a caption "Now, would you like it in a box from a 1,000-year-old tree ..." when (a) most boxes made in Canada are from board that's 100% recycled content and (b) any trees that are used from Canadian forests would most likely be less than 100 years old.[15]
- The *Globe and Mail* newspaper runs an article with the headline: "Is there an 800-year-old tree in your toilet paper?" when, in fact, 60% of the toilet paper made in Canada is recycled content, and as noted above (yet again!) most trees in Canada are less than 100 years old.[16]

Chapter 2
Boreal Forest
Let's be really clear what we are talking about

I am not sure when I first heard or saw the word *boreal* but I certainly remember the first time I saw the aurora borealis, the Northern Lights. I was standing by a lake in Saskatchewan, Canada, and those dancing, prancing green lights in the night sky were just magical.[1]

I may be completely wrong about this, but I suspect most Canadians (who live in cities) have not personally seen "the lights" and don't really know much about "the boreal" itself. It's forest somewhere north of Steeles, isn't it? Or maybe Barrie these days?[2]

The Canadian boreal zone and forest are, in fact, world treasures teeming with birdlife and wildlife and of huge global significance as a carbon sink and store. In our own self-interest, we need to conserve and protect them. Having said that, it is very important to understand exactly what is meant by *boreal* when we hear claims that it is under threat or being destroyed.

Is it the boreal zone that is being "destroyed," and if so, all of it or just part of it? Is it the world's boreal forests that are "threatened"? Or is it the management of a specific boreal forest that's being called into question? These distinctions are especially important when statistics are used in support of environmental claims. Which specific boreal area is actually being talked about, and do the statistics being used actually apply to them? Here are some key clarifications.

The Boreal Zone (Also known as the Circumpolar Zone)
Scientists have divided the world into four broad climatic domains, zones, or biomes: tropical, subtropical, temperate, and boreal.[3] The boreal zone covers 1.9 billion hectares (4.7 billion acres), stretching in a band below the North Pole. Most of it is in the Russian Federation (60%) and Canada

(28%), but it is also found in parts of the United States, China, Finland, Greenland, Iceland, Kazakhstan, Mongolia, Norway and Sweden.[4]

When people claim the boreal is being "threatened" or "destroyed," you first need to clarify if they mean the whole of the boreal zone (stretching across the countries noted above) or just part of it. Concerns about the fate of the Siberian tiger, for example, obviously relate only to the state of the boreal zone in the Russian Federation.

The North American Boreal Zone
This is obviously a more specific geographic term, covering the boreal climatic domain located in Alaska and the provinces and territories of Canada. It covers some 627 million hectares (88% of it in Canada).

The Canadian Boreal Zone
This is even more specific (excluding the boreal zone in Alaska) and amounts to 552 million hectares. The zone comprises 270 million hectares of forest; 39 million hectares of semi-boreal or transitional wooded land; 171 million hectares of other land including some with tree cover; and 71 million hectares of lakes, ponds, and rivers.[5] About 96% of it is owned by Canadian federal, provincial or territorial governments.

The Canadian Boreal Forest
This is specifically boreal forest land, a subset of the Canadian boreal zone mentioned above, comprising some 270 million hectares of forest, 70% of which is left as wilderness (unmanaged). Canada's total forest lands comprise some 12 distinct terrestrial ecozones, with boreal forest prominent in seven of them: the Taiga Plains, Taiga Shield, Boreal Shield, Boreal Plains, Taiga Cordillera, Boreal Cordillera, and Hudson Plains. [6]

The Canadian boreal forest (sometimes branded as the Amazon of the North) is often cited by environmental groups as being under threat from industrial logging. Let's have a closer look at how some of these claims are framed.

In a recent campaign against the use of virgin pulp to make toilet paper, the New York based Natural Resources Defense Council (NRDC) and STAND.earth claimed that:

"Much of the tissue pulp in the United States comes from the boreal forest of Canada. This vast landscape of coniferous, birch, and aspen trees contains some of the last of the world's remaining intact forests, as well as boreal caribou, pine marten, and billions of songbirds. Yet, industrial logging claims more than a million acres of boreal forest every year, equivalent to seven National Hockey League rinks each minute, in part to meet demand for tissue products in the United States." [7]

The overall impression here is of a rapacious industry levelling seven National Hockey League (NHL) rinks a minute. *Terrible!* And this emotive image is repeated continuously in subsequent NRDC blogs by author Jennifer Skene, aided and abetted by an echo chamber led by, among others, Canadian broadcaster David Suzuki.[8]

There is a deception here. On the one hand, there is the "vast landscape" of the boreal and on the other, the million acres logged. The "vast landscape" of the Canadian boreal forest, as noted above, comprises some 270 million hectares of forest. The 270 million hectares converts to 667 million acres, by my count.

What NRDC is *not saying*, then, is that only 1 million acres out of 667 million acres is being harvested. *That's a mere 0.15% of the boreal!* The

Canadian boreal forest is "threatened by industrial logging" that occurs on only 0.15% of it! Or a mere 2% over the past 15 years. Strange how the facts give a totally different impression.

It is also worth noting that most of the harvest is for lumber (not for tissue) and that, by law, this area must be successfully regenerated after harvest (see **TOILET PAPER**).

Chapter 3

Cardboard
Technically, cardboard doesn't exist!

To most of us, *cardboard* just means a brown box that's used to deliver stuff to our homes or workplaces. We see the word displayed in large letters on recycling bins in strip malls. Or when our local municipality reminds us to put our corrugated cardboard out to the curb on recycling day.

There's absolutely nothing wrong with effective communication to a target audience. And there's a reasonable argument to be made that we don't really need to know too much detail, that there's enough clutter out there already. We all *know* what a cardboard box is.

At the same time, however, the use of the word *cardboard* does create confusion in some circumstances. For, technically, cardboard doesn't exist. The box we are talking about is either a *corrugated* box or it is a *boxboard* or *paperboard* carton. What's the difference, and why does it matter?

Corrugated Box
A corrugated box is made from strong paper fibres, primarily because it is used as a shipping container designed in most cases to deliver many similar products. It comprises several layers of paper fibre to give it that strength: a top and bottom layer (linerboard) and a middle layer (corrugating medium). The wavy, ripple-like shape of the medium in the middle gives the box its strength. Think of the curve of a strong Roman arch or a corrugated tin roof. A corrugated box *always* has this ripple layer in the middle.

Boxboard or Paperboard Carton
A boxboard or paperboard carton, on the other hand, does not require the same strength properties as a corrugated box because it normally holds just a single item. Here's a good example to illustrate the difference: Your

favourite cereal box is usually made from boxboard or paperboard, but 20 or 30 of those cereal boxes were delivered to the retailer in just one stronger corrugated box.

Why Does the Difference Matter?

To most people, both types of boxes are simply cardboard and the difference doesn't really matter that much.[1] But it matters to recyclers who want to turn the used cardboard into a new paper product. Like a chef, they need to know the properties of their various ingredients. They need to mix and match paper fibre strengths to make sure that whatever new paper product they are recycling it into will work in practice. Too many thin used fibres by themselves might not be strong enough. So, it's important for recyclers to know how much of that bale of cardboard collected for recycling is actually corrugated boxes (or old corrugated containers, OCC), old boxboard (*OBB*), or just mixed residential paper (household paper all thrown together). They need to get the furnish (or recipe) right.

Making the distinction between corrugated and boxboard is also important from a waste management policy perspective. Lumping corrugated and boxboard into one category called *cardboard* in waste audits and other data-gathering exercises makes it a lot harder to determine recycling rates and to target recycling efforts at specific waste-paper streams.

Left: Corrugated board has a ripple. Right: Cereal in boxboard on top of a stronger corrugated box used to deliver many cereal boxes.

So, when you go home tonight, or if you are already at home, check out that brown box in your basement, garage, or kitchen. And remember, *it ain't cardboard!*

Chapter 4
Deforestation
Confronting the confusion and the big green lie

For years Canadians have been fed the big green lie that deforestation is a major issue. *It isn't*. The Canadian deforestation rate is well below 1%, among the lowest in the world.[1]

That's not to say that deforestation isn't a key global concern. *It is*. Or that Canadians do not share some responsibility for consuming palm oil, soy, and cattle and wood products provided by supply chains linked to deforestation in other countries. *They do*. Or that we can't do better. *We can*.

Unfortunately, there is widespread public (and media) confusion about what deforestation is and what it isn't. From a dictionary point of view, it would be easy to conclude that deforestation is simply about removing trees, and that reforestation is about growing them back again.[2] That's what the commonly displayed images all show: a stark clear-cut, or a young green spruce stretching skyward.

But for people whose job it is to track deforestation and to do something about it, it's a lot more complicated than that. For starters, there is a major difference between forest cover loss and deforestation. Put simply, forest cover loss includes *all* causes of forest loss: *natural* disturbances such as fire, insect infestations, and natural tree death; as well as *human-induced* disturbances like the conversion of forest land to agriculture and so on.

Deforestation *only* includes the last part: when forest land is used for a maize crop, a hydro reservoir, a mine, an oil and gas development, or a residential subdivision, for example. The confusion over where forest cover loss and deforestation begin and end has led to a lot of sloppy journalism, false headlines, and misleading claims about deforestation that continue to this day (see **FOREST COVER** and **EXAGGERATION**).

Change of land use

The world's forest scientists have debated for decades about how to define deforestation, finally deciding that it basically means "a change of land use from forest land to non-forest land." This is something they can track over time and do something about.

> **UN Definition of Deforestation:** the conversion of forest to other land use independently whether human-induced or not.
> *Explanatory notes:*
> 1. Includes permanent reduction of the tree canopy cover below the minimum 10 percent threshold.
> 2. It includes areas of forest converted to agriculture, pasture, water reservoirs, mining and urban areas.
> 3. The term specifically excludes areas where the trees have been removed as a result of harvesting or logging, and where the forest is expected to regenerate naturally or with the aid of silvicultural measures.
> 4. The term also includes areas where, for example, the impact of disturbance, over-utilization or changing environmental conditions affects the forest to an extent that it cannot sustain a canopy cover above the 10 percent threshold.
>
> Source: *Global Forest Resources Assessment*, 2020.

This is not just an "industry" or a Canadian or US government definition of *deforestation*, as some environmental advocates and media claim. It is how 236 nations report data to the Food and Agriculture Organization of the United Nations (FAO) on a regular basis so that global and individual country rates of deforestation can be uniformly tracked in a common format, assessments made, and remedial action taken.

And this national and global tracking exercise also includes guidelines on how countries should measure deforestation. The FAO, for example, makes a key distinction between the *permanent* disturbance of forest land (where the land is deforested and not coming back to forest) and the *temporary* disturbance of forest land (such as fire, insect infestations, and the harvesting of trees for lumber and paper).

Forest that has been harvested is expected to revert to forest through either *natural* regeneration (as it's done for thousands of years) or *artificial* regeneration (tree planting or direct seeding) within a certain period of time. This is why logging is not considered to be deforestation. As long as forest land remains forest land and is not converted to agriculture, pasture, mining, hydro-electric development, or residential subdivisions and so on, it is not considered to be deforested.

So, how are we doing globally, and how are we doing in Canada and the United States? [3]

Global deforestation

The bad news is that the world is estimated to have lost some 420 million hectares of forest through deforestation over the past 30 years. The good news is that the rate of loss is declining. "Deforestation occurred at a rate of 15.8 million hectares per year in 1990 to 2000; 15.1 million hectares per year in 2000 to 2010; 11.8 million hectares in 2010 to 2015; and 10.2 million hectares per year in 2015 to 2020."[4]

Forest Expansion and Deforestation

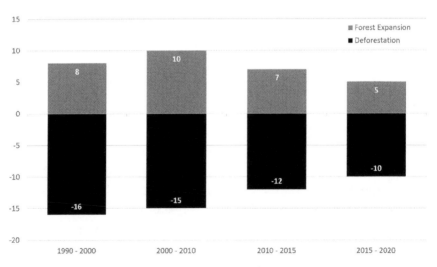

Source: *Global Forest Resources Assessment*, 2020.

More than 90% of this deforestation has occurred in the tropical climatic domain, where forest has been removed for the growing of agricultural crops, soy and palm oil, timber and pulp, or cleared for cattle grazing and wood fuel.[5] The highest annual deforestation rate between 2015 and 2020 was in Africa, followed by South America and Asia.[6]

In its latest report, the FAO notes that although the quality of deforestation data supplied by individual countries is good and higher than in previous assessments, major gaps and deficiencies still remain.[7] With that caution very much in mind, here is a list of the deforestation rates of the 16 "best performing" countries, based on the reports those countries made to the FAO for its latest assessment. The full list can be found in **APPENDIX 1**.

Best Performing Countries

Country	% Forest Land Deforested
Norway	0.05
Sweden	0.05
Belarus	0.04
Spain	0.02
Bhutan	0.02
Vietnam	0.01
Mongolia	0.01
Latvia	0.01
CANADA	0.01
Poland	0.01
Lithuania	0.01
Turkey	0.01
Croatia	0.01
Serbia	0.01
Ukraine	0.01
Romania	0.01

Source: Global Forest Resources Assessment, 2020.

How are the United States and Canada doing?

The United States didn't actually provide a specific deforestation number for the period 2015 to 2020 in its latest country report to the FAO. It stated that data collection changes in the Western United States had complicated things so the reporting table was left blank. "To fill the table would have resulted (in creating) a false impression of deforestation that has not occurred."[8]

Canada's deforestation rate was 0.01% in 2018 (see endnote 1) reflecting a slight decline over the years. More recent numbers (from Canada's National Inventory Report to the United Nations) indicate an increase in forest conversion to both agriculture and what are called settlements in 2019, but the overall deforestation rate still remains at 0.01%.[9]

Historically, the major cause of deforestation in Canada has been the conversion of forest land to agriculture and, to a lesser extent, spikes in hydro-electric development.[10] Contrary to public perception, the forest industry's contribution to overall deforestation in Canada is minimal (just 4%), primarily through the creation of new permanent forest access roads.

Major causes of deforestation in Canada

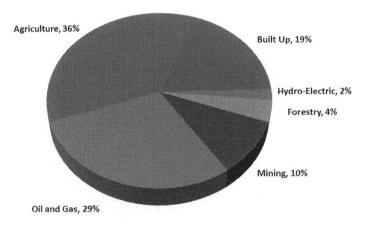

Note: 'Built Up' incudes industrial, institutional, commercial and municipal urban development; recreation (ski hills and golf courses); and transportation. Forestry is mainly the creation of permanent forest access roads.

Source: Natural Resources Canada.

A definitional debate

In late 2019, the Wildlands League produced a study of logging scars in part of the province of Ontario, claiming that this was de facto deforestation and that Canada in general was greatly understating its deforestation performance. Several environmental groups have seized on this study to question the accuracy of Canada's reported numbers.

The logging scars in question arise from what are called landing areas where full trees are sometimes dragged from the stump to the roadside so that merchantable logs can be separated from the waste wood. Over many years, decades actually, these particular landing areas have not sufficiently reverted to forest and for that, the provincial forest ministry that owns the land is clearly responsible.

That issue aside, the study has raised questions about how deforestation is measured and whether its findings can be extrapolated beyond the area studied. Forestry experts say that extrapolating estimates from 27 study sites in one region to the total harvest area of Ontario is problematic.

That's because most of these study sites were harvested using full-tree harvesting two or even three decades ago when stroke delimbers first came into use. Today, waste wood (tops and branches) is piled and burned instead, or chipped for pulp and energy in a nearby mill. It should also be noted that not all harvested areas in Ontario are forests that have never been harvested before. The forest losses claimed in the study, then, should not be extrapolated to the whole of Ontario, and especially not to those areas that already have an existing road network.

There's a reason why these landing areas are not included in Ontario's deforestation estimates in the first place. They are on *forest* land, and deforestation technically occurs only when forest land is converted to non-forest land. They are also *small* areas, and Canada follows the Intergovernmental Panel on Climate Change (IPCC) guidelines on measuring those too.[11]

Any small "change events" (less than 1 hectare in size, such as landings) are to be excluded from deforestation estimates. A few smaller European countries have chosen to adopt smaller minimal areas (0.5 hectare) but this level of detail is just not economically or practically feasible in a country the size of Canada. This exclusion of small areas works both ways, however. If *new* forest is added, but the area is not large enough to meet the size guidelines, it too is excluded from the estimates.[12]

Chapter 5

"Degraded" Forest
What exactly is it, and how do you measure it?

It's easy to label a forest or a country's forests as degraded. It's much harder to actually measure that degradation. How do you do it? And where do you start? Because there's no such thing as a perfect forest (see **PRISTINE AND UNDISTURBED FOREST**).

Nature is a continuous cycle of decay and regeneration punctuated by disturbances (earthquakes, volcanoes, avalanches, wind storms, fire, droughts, floods, insects and disease) long before any human-induced impacts need to be considered.

And then there are related terms such as *decline, desertification, fragmentation*[1]. Where do they fit in? Some definitions of forest degradation emphasize biodiversity conservation and carbon sequestration. Others focus on wood production, soil cover depth and fertility, recreation and cultural needs.

How can you possibly cover all these different things under one definition? And then there's the question of degree: Is the impact of the degradation light, moderate, or strong? Is it reversible or irreversible? It really does make a difference. And what is the objective? Conservation and protection of the forest ecosystem? The sustainable harvest of the forest? Both? [2]

You can see why coming up with a broadly accepted definition of forest degradation has proven so difficult. The Food and Agriculture Organization of the United Nations (FAO) recently surveyed 236 member countries on that very question.[3] The results were telling. Yes, I waded through every single response!

The UN members were first asked if they monitored degraded forest. Some 25 countries (or 10%) either ignored the question or did not respond.[4]

Do you monitor degraded forest?

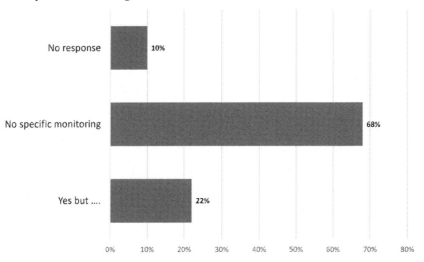

Source: *Analysis of 236 Country Reports to Global Forest Resources Assessment*, 2020.

The majority (160 countries or 68%, including Canada) said no, they did not specifically monitor forest degradation. *Only 51 countries (22%)* said they monitored the area of degraded forest, although the extent of that monitoring seems a little wishy-washy in light of some of the answers to the questions that followed.

The countries were asked for their national definition of degraded forest and to describe their monitoring results. Most didn't have a national definition; some said they were "working on" one; while others offered very general forest policy statements and achievements. A few quoted clauses from the Kyoto Protocol or suggestions on defining forest degradation arising from the Convention on Biological Diversity (CBD).

For its part, the United States said it followed the Kyoto Protocol definition: "A direct human induced long-term loss (persisting for X years or more) of at least Y % of forest carbon stocks (and forest values) since time T and not qualifying as deforestation or an elected activity under Article 3.4 of the Kyoto Protocol (Schoene *et al* 2007) and (Mollicone and Souza 2007)."

It noted, however, that it doesn't directly measure degraded forest. "But we do measure the components necessary to calculate some degradation matrix of the sort described in Lund 2009." This is a reference to Gyde Lund's 2009 article "What is a Degraded Forest?" the white paper on definitions of degradation he prepared for the FAO (see endnote 2).

The US response gets to the heart of the issue. There is no one agreed-upon definition of what a degraded forest is, but it is possible to monitor and track individual components of what could be called degradation: loss of biodiversity, carbon accounting, soil cover depth and fertility.

The 12 countries of the Montreal Process, for example, including Canada and the United States, regularly report progress on sustainability indicators such as biological diversity; ecosystem productive capacity, health and vitality; the conservation of soil and water resources; and the forest's contribution to carbon cycles. The countries of the Montreal Process represent 90% of the world's temperate and boreal forests.[5] Why not build on what they are doing?

See also **DEFORESTATION, FOREST, FOREST COVER, PRISTINE AND UNDISTURBED FOREST** and **SUSTAINABLE**.

UN Sustainable Development Goals:
15.3 By 2030, combat deserticication, restore degraded land and soil, including land affected by desertification, drought and floods, and strive to achieve a land degradation-neutral world.
(15.3.1) Proportion of land that is degraded over total land area.

Aichi Biodiversity Target 5: By 2020, the rate of loss of all natural habitats, including forests, is at least halved and where feasible brought close to zero, and degradation and fragmentation is significantly reduced.

UN Strategic Plan for Forests Goal 1: Reverse the loss of forest cover worldwide through sustainable forest management, including protection, restoration, afforestation and reforestation, and increase efforts to prevent forest degradation and contribute to the global effort of addressing climate change.

Chapter 6

Environmentally Friendly, Eco-Friendly
Avoid these terms. They mean nothing!

Your BS detector should be ringing loudly and its red lights flashing every time you see these terms. Without more detail and back-up information, they mean absolutely nothing. And yet they are extremely common, a short-hand sales and marketing pitch to persuade you that this product is better than another.

There are guidelines for backing up eco-friendly claims. Just saying that a new copy paper is "more environmentally friendly than harvesting trees" or that a food packaging item is an "eco-friendly replacement for polystyrene, plastics, and tree-based paper products" is not enough.

Eco-Friendly, 400 Pack

An environmentally friendly alternative to single-use plastics, paper or foam tableware.

For a claim to be treated seriously, it must offer consumers an explanatory statement or a description of the methods used to make the comparisons. Results from a published standard or recognized test method, and details on the assumptions made in the comparisons, should be offered.

If they are not, then you would seem to have a clear breach of the environmental advertising and labelling guidelines established by the appropriate US and Canadian authorities (the Federal Trade Commission

(FTC)[1] and the Competition Bureau of Canada)[2]. *Don't buy it, and complain to the company selling the product, and to the authorities cited in the* **ENDNOTES** *and the* **KEY SOURCES** *(the FTC and the Competition Bureau of Canada) at the back of the book.*

Chapter 7

Exaggeration
Inflated claims and emotional branding

Here's a short summary of some of the exaggerated claims made elsewhere in the book.

1. What does Xmas wrapping paper have to do with 100,000 elephants?
I kid you not! Some media would have you believe that Canadians dump the equivalent weight of 100,000 elephants of wrapping paper after Christmas. *Not so!* The so-called "study" that everybody quotes from does not, in fact, exist. And any other data that's floating around is at least 17 years old! See **XMAS PAPER** for the full story about this incredibly sloppy journalism.

2. What do you mean 99.8% of the Canadian boreal is not logged?
Logging operations in Canada's boreal forest are "widespread" according to a recent report from the New York based Natural Resources Defense Council (NRDC) and STAND.earth. *Widespread?* Harvesting a mere 0.15% of the boreal a year amounts to "widespread"? Just 2% over the past 15 years? Must be the new math. See **BOREAL FOREST** and **TOILET PAPER**.

3. Three billion sounds impressive but what does it mean?
Vancouver-based environmental group Canopy claims that 3 billion trees "disappear into packaging" every year. It would be interesting to see how they count that. Does one large tree equal 20 spindly ones? Are the trees from previously unlogged forests, or are they from forests that have been replanted by logging companies? Was the forest harvested for lumber with just the leftover sawmill residues (wood chips, shavings and sawdust) used for packaging grades? We don't know, and Canopy doesn't say.

But even if the 3 billion guesstimate is in the ballpark, it represents less than half of 1% of what's in US forests (365 billion trees). The North American boreal supposedly has 500 billion trees; and if an International Boreal Conservation Campaign video is right, there are some 600 billion trees in the Canadian boreal forest alone! And that's not counting the rest of the world's forests! See **"TREE-FREE."**

Above: slide from a recent International Boreal Conservation campaign video.

4. Now for the truth serum on the Blue Box program.

Politicians like to promote high recycling targets (70%, 80%, and more) to encourage greater diversion of waste from landfill. And if possible, they like those recycling rates to be higher than those of the previous administration or a neighbouring jurisdiction. People "love their Blue Boxes" and we want them to feel good about "doing something for the environment" are the usual refrains.

Which is all well and good until you run into the realities of recycling in North America: that sending stuff to landfill is usually cheaper; and that what is sent on for recycling by consumers is just the beginning of the journey. Contamination and the remanufacturing process, unfortunately, mean that a lot of material never ends up in a new product.

If you were to take into account the contamination in the bales that the end-markets receive and have to landfill or burn, plus the specific material characteristics that reduce process yields when remanufacturing used materials, then the *real recycling rate* for Ontario's much-vaunted

Blue Box program, for example, could be just over 30%, not the 57% it is currently reporting and definitely not the 75% to 80% that the politicians are hoping, or conning us into believing, will be achieved someday soon. Despite all that, the claim that "Recycling is dead" is also total BS. See **RECYCLING** and **RECOVERY AND RECYCLING RATES.**

Is the real recycling rate of Ontario's much-vaunted Blue Box only 32%?

5. Sorry, folks, but post-consumer recycled content is no "better" than pre-consumer.

Post-consumer recycled content is being held up by some people as an environmental gold standard. In fact, it's really the same material just coming from different places along the feedstock supply chain.

It's no more "circular" than pre-consumer, and both replace virgin material. Indeed, it could be argued that pre-consumer recycled content is environmentally superior. It requires a lot less energy to collect, sort, clean, and transform than post-consumer material, which tends to be more contaminated. See **RECYCLED CONTENT.**

6. David Suzuki is dead wrong on paper recycling.

Canadian broadcaster and author David Suzuki recently claimed that paper products were "barely recycled" in Canada. He couldn't be more wrong. In fact, more than 90% of the raw materials used by the Canadian pulp and paper industry are sawmill residues and recycled paper.[1] According to the World Business Council for Sustainable Development, North America's overall paper recovery rate is almost 70%, one of the highest in the world.[2]

In Statistics Canada's bi-annual survey of waste diversion, paper leads all other materials, representing almost 40% of Canada's total recycling effort.[3] And on the packaging front, Suzuki is obviously ignorant of the fact that most Canadian packaging is not made from virgin material at all. Most of it is 100% recycled content. The recovery rate for old corrugated boxes in Ontario's Blue Box program, for example, has been 98% four years running. For more details see "Suzuki dead wrong on paper's circular economy."[4]

7. Headlines gave a totally false impression about deforestation.

The media screwed up big time in 2014, and the resulting confusion is still with us today. Back then, the non-profit World Resources Institute (WRI), working with Global Forest Watch, Greenpeace, and the University of Maryland, produced a study that claimed that 8% of the world's intact forest landscapes (large undeveloped forest areas showing no signs of human activity) had been degraded between 2000 and 2013.

The largest areas of degradation were in the northern boreal forest belt of Canada, Russia and Alaska; in tropical forest regions such as the Amazon; and in the Congo basin. Three countries (Canada, Russia, and Brazil) together contained 65% of the world's remaining such forest and were responsible for more than half its degradation, according to the study. Canada, it said, led the world in the amount of degradation.[5]

The Canadian media, in particular, leapt upon this news, and ran damning headlines: "Canada largest contributor to deforestation worldwide," "Deforestation worse than Brazil, Canada is now the world's leading 'deforestation nation'," and "Canada surpasses Brazil as global leader in deforestation."[6]

The misleading headlines were totally false. For starters, the word *deforestation* does not even appear in the WRI press release announcing the study results. The study is actually about something different: forest cover loss. Forest cover loss includes *all* causes of forest loss (fire, insect infestations, natural tree death, plus the "deforestation" parts: the clearing of forest for agriculture, pasture, hydro-electric development, residential subdivisions and so on).

**Canada Largest Contributor To
Deforestation Worldwide: Study**

The Huffington Post Canada

**Canada is now the world's leading
'deforestation nation'**
Stephen Leahy
October 1, 2014 ENVIRONMENT

Canada surpasses Brazil as global leader in
deforestation
Posted September 16, 2014 by Common Sense Canadian in Canada

The authors of the study acknowledged this: that fire was the most significant cause of forest cover loss in the boreal;[7] and that beetle infestations played a key role in Canada's forest cover loss over the period.[8] The headlines and text in various media, however, gave a totally false impression about deforestation that lingers to this day.[9] See **DEFORESTATION, "DEGRADED" FOREST,** and **FOREST COVER.**

Chapter 8

Forest

Navigating the confusing mix of terms and definitions

When you are being asked to donate money to preserve "ancient" forests it is kind of useful to know whether they actually exist or not (see "ANCIENT" FORESTS). Or when you are told the Canadian boreal is being "ravaged" and "rapidly clear-cut" it's helpful to know how much is actually being harvested and regenerated there (see **BOREAL FOREST**). Add in words like **PRISTINE AND UNDISTURBED FOREST, "DEGRADED" FOREST** and **"OLD-GROWTH"**, and it's no wonder people are confused.

So many terms are used to describe forests (*natural, virgin, primeval, original, ancient, primary, pristine, degraded, plantation, old-growth*) that it's very confusing and sometimes even emotionally draining just to discuss them. It also makes it harder to gather appropriate data on them, and to ensure that they retain their health and vitality.

The world's forest scientists through the Food and Agriculture Organization of the United Nations (FAO) have wrestled with these definitional issues for decades, and will continue to struggle. After all, there are more than 60,000 different species of tree[1] and many, many definitions of forest. For the moment, and into the foreseeable future, the FAO has settled on two major categories of forest: **naturally regenerating forest** and **planted forest.**

The big picture

The world currently has some 4.06 billion hectares of forest spread over four climatic domains: tropical, boreal, temperate, and subtropical. Most of it (93%) is naturally generating forest, the balance is planted forest.

Each of these two main categories has sub-categories. About one-third of the naturally regenerating forest, for example, is what's called **primary** forest. The FAO describes this as comprising native tree species with no clearly visible indications of human activity, and where ecological processes are not significantly disturbed. Most of this primary forest (61%) is in three countries (Brazil, Canada and the United States). And over the past 30 years, some 7% of it (81 million hectares) has been lost, mainly through its conversion to agriculture (see **DEFORESTATION**).

The 7% of the world's forest that is planted is divided into **plantation forests** (3%) and **other planted forests** (4%). The plantation sub-category is intensively managed, composed of one or two tree species, native or exotic, of equal age, and planted with regular spacing. Much of the other planted subcategory is forest established for ecosystem restoration and the protection of soil and water.[2]

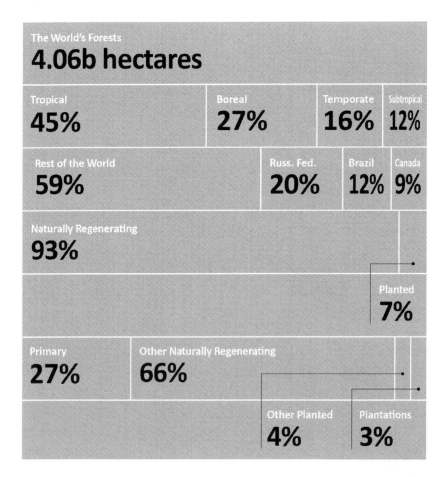

United States and Canada

Some significant differences exist between the forests of Canada and of the United States, primarily because of their respective geographies. Canada's forests are predominantly boreal (77%) while US forests are mostly temperate and tropical with some boreal forest in Alaska.

Canada has 12% more forest land than the United States, 16% more naturally generating forest, and almost three times as much primary forest. The United States, on the other hand, has 67% more non-primary or "other naturally regenerating" forest than Canada, and slightly less than twice as much planted forest[3].

It should be pointed out that the data supplied by countries to the FAO, especially of primary forest areas, are estimates based on extrapolations from multiple sources and methodologies. While there may be *academic* agreement on a definition of primary forest, there is not yet an *operational* one. Canada, for example, does not have original data on primary forest, and

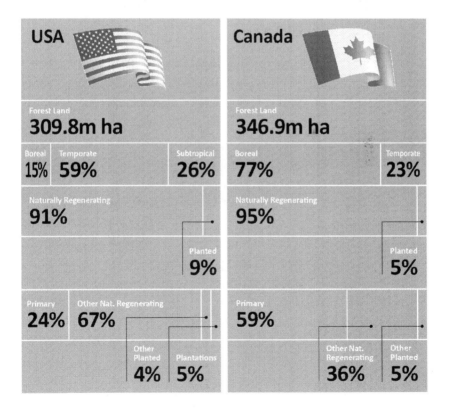

does not "have high confidence in the reported primary forest area trend."[4]

It should also be pointed out that the annual tree harvest of both countries is relatively small: 0.2% in Canada and less than 2.0% in the United States.[5]

Key Definitions[6]

naturally regenerating forest (category): Forest predominantly composed of trees established through natural regeneration.

- Includes forests for which it is not possible to distinguish whether planted or naturally generated.
- Includes forests with a mix of naturally generated native tree species and planted/seeded trees, and where the naturally regenerated trees are expected to constitute the major part of the growing stock at stand maturity.
- Includes coppice from trees originally established through natural regeneration.
- Includes naturally regenerated trees of introduced species.

primary forest (subcategory): Naturally regenerated forest of native tree species, where there are no clearly visible indications of human activities and the ecological processes are not significantly disturbed.

- Includes both pristine and managed forests that meet the definition.
- Includes forests where Indigenous peoples engage in traditional forest stewardship activities that meet the definition.
- Includes forests with visible signs of abiotic damages (such as storm, snow, drought) and biotic damages (such as insects, pests, and diseases).
- Excludes forests where hunting, poaching, trapping or gathering have caused significant native species loss or disturbance to ecological processes.
- Some key characteristics of primary forests:
    - They show natural forest dynamics, such as natural tree species composition, occurrence of dead wood, natural age structure and natural regeneration processes

- The area is large enough to maintain its natural ecological processes
- There has been no known significant human intervention or the last significant human intervention was long enough ago to have allowed the natural species composition and processes to have become re-established.

planted forest (**category**): Forest predominantly composed of trees established through planting and/or deliberate seeding.

- In this context, *predominantly* means that the planted/seeded trees are expected to constitute more than 50% of the growing stock at maturity.
- Includes coppice from trees that were originally planted or seeded.

plantation forest (subcategory): Planted forest that is intensively managed and meets all of the following criteria at planting and stand maturity: one or two species, even age class, and regular spacing.

- Specifically includes short rotation plantation for wood, fibre and energy.
- Specifically excludes forest planted for protection or ecosystem restoration.
- Specifically excludes forest established through planting or seeding which at stand maturity resembles or will resemble naturally regenerating forest.

Other planted forest (subcategory): Planted forest that is not classified as plantation forest.

See also **"ANCIENT" FORESTS, BOREAL FOREST, "DEGRADED" FOREST, "OLD-GROWTH" FOREST,** and **PRISTINE AND UNDISTURBED FOREST.**

Chapter 9

Forest Cover
Are we running out of trees?

We hear all sorts of bad news about the state of the world's forests. They are threatened, endangered, and being destroyed. Deforestation is rampant. The Amazon rainforest is on the way out. The Canadian boreal is next.

There are some elements of truth behind the dire warnings, especially with climate change ramping up. But how much is fear-mongering and how much is real? In the instant clamour of social media and the loud voices of self-appointed experts, it is sometimes hard to tell. So let's check the best data we can get our hands on, and go from there.

According to the United Nations Food and Agriculture Organization (FAO), which has been collecting and interpreting data on the world's forests since 1946, we currently have just over 4 billion hectares (10 billion acres) of forest spread across four climatic domains (tropical, boreal, temperate and subtropical). The overwhelming majority of this forest (93%) regenerates naturally. The balance is planted forest (3% of it in plantations).[1]

The bad news is that over the past 30 years some 178 million hectares (440 million acres) of global forest land have disappeared,[2] lost primarily through the conversion of forest land to agriculture. Between 2010 and 2020, the net loss of forest area was 4.7 million hectares per year, although this is a considerable improvement on previous years.[3] Based on recent history, though, the FAO says the world is "not on track to meet the UN's Strategic Plan for Forests to increase forest area by 3% worldwide by 2030."[4]

The good news is that the rate of loss has slowed down, "mainly because of reduced deforestation in some countries, plus increases in forest area in others through afforestation (the planting of forest where none existed before) and the natural expansion of forests."[5]

Annual forest area net change, by decade and region, 1990–2020

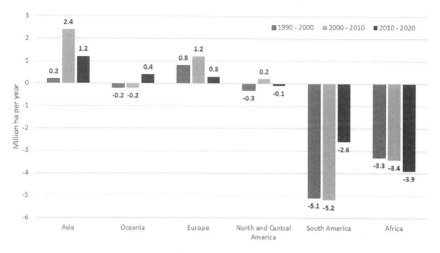

Source: *Global Forest Resources Assessment 2020 Key Findings.*

The highest net loss of forest area over the past 10 years has been in Africa (3.9 million hectares), followed by South America (2.6 million hectares), with Africa showing an increasing trend of net loss and South America a declining trend.

Asia had the highest net gain in forest area, followed by Oceania and Europe (which includes the Russian Federation). North and Central America have been pretty steady.

Which brings us to the United States and Canada. Canada has 347 million hectares of forest land: enough to fill all of Japan, Italy, Cambodia, Nicaragua, France, Germany, Ghana, Cameroon, Sweden, South Korea and Uruguay with still enough trees left over to fill the United Kingdom. Canada's forest area has been stable, losing less than half of 1% (0.4%) over the past 28 years.[6]

Forest area in the United States has also remained stable since 1990. In fact, it increased by 2.4% or 18 million acres to reach 765.5 million acres (309.8 million hectares) in 2017.[7] A paper industry association says that's an area equivalent to more than 1,200 NFL football fields every day.[8]

See also **FORESTS, DEFORESTATION, "DEGRADED" FOREST, PRISTINE AND UNDISTURBED FOREST.**

Global annual forest area net change, by decade, 1990–2020

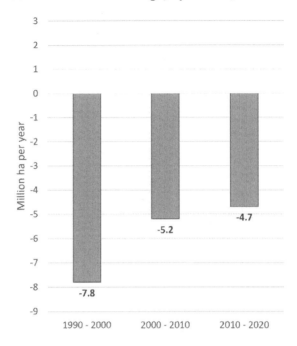

Source: *Global Forest Resources Assessment 2020 Key Findings.*

Key UN Definitions[9]

forest expansion (category): Expansion of forest on land that until then was under a different land use. It implies a change in land use, from non-forest land to forest land. Its two sub-categories are:

- **afforestation** (subcategory): Where forest is established through planting and/or deliberate seeding on land that until then was under a different land use.
- **natural expansion** (subcategory): Expansion of forest through natural succession on land that until then was under a different land use. Again, it implies a transformation of land use from non-forest to forest (e.g., forest succession on land previously used for agriculture).

deforestation:[10] The conversion of forest to other land use independently of whether this was human-induced or not.

- It includes permanent reduction of the tree canopy cover below a minimum 10% threshold in areas of forest converted to agriculture, pasture, water reservoirs, mining and urban areas.
- It specifically excludes areas where the trees have been removed as a result of harvesting or logging, and where the forest is expected to regenerate naturally or with the aid of silvicultural measures.
- The term also includes areas where, for example, the impact of disturbance, over-utilization, or changing environmental conditions affects the forest to an extent that it cannot sustain a canopy cover above the 10% threshold.

net change (in forest area): The forest area net change is the difference in forest area between two Forest Resource Assessment (FRA) reference years (say, between 2010 and 2020). The net change can be either positive (gain), negative (loss), or zero (no change).

Chapter 10

Fresh Trees Are Needed Because Paper Is In Landfill
Misleading

This claim assumes that there is a *direct connection* between paper ending up in landfill and the need to harvest fresh trees. While it is true that the overall paper life cycle requires fresh (virgin) paper fibres to be introduced at some point in the system to keep the whole paper cycle going,[1] it is *not true* that paper products ending up in landfill *automatically* require the harvesting of fresh trees to supply new feedstock.

That's because paper recovery in North America is close to 70% and more and more paper products are being made with recycled content.[2] So, for those products incorporating recycled content, you don't need replacement virgin material, you don't need to cut down more trees, you just need more recovered paper to recycle.

Most Canadian packaging mills, for example, make 100% recycled content board using old boxes and paper collected from the back of factories and supermarkets, from office buildings, and from residential Blue Box programs.[3] Sometimes they have to import recovered fibre from the Northern United States so that the mills can keep operating. But these particular mills do not use freshly cut trees. In fact, they physically *cannot* use freshly cut trees because they don't have the necessary tools to process them, such as debarking, chipping, and pulping equipment.

The notion of someone grabbing a chainsaw and heading for the forest to make a new box because someone has dumped an old box in landfill, is totally false.

So, the notion of someone grabbing a

chainsaw and heading for the nearest forest to make a new box because someone has dumped an old box in landfill, is totally false. And while it is impossible to know how much paper in landfill is virgin or recycled fibre, with the worldwide increase in the use of recycled fibre there's a good chance that more of it is recycled than virgin.[4] In fact, given the nature of the paper life cycle, those fibres may have been used many times over already.[5]

See also **"KILLING" AND "SAVING" TREES.**

Chapter 11

Generation (Of Waste)
Does not mean the waste was dumped!

This is one of the most frustrating media boo-boos around. And it's not entirely the media's fault!

When a government document says that so many tons (or tonnes) of solid waste were *generated* by a particular province or state or country, it's often interpreted that the same amount of material was sent on to landfill. *This is not true!*

The word *generated* in waste terms means the total amount of what's left over from consuming a product. For example, you drink a bottle or carton of milk. Your body deals with the milk (*liquid* waste), but the bottle or carton is left over (solid waste). That's the generated solid waste, what's left over: the starting point. It doesn't mean that all the milk bottles or cartons went to landfill or incineration because many of them, in fact, may very well have been recycled or composted.

Consumers, unfortunately, are frequently misled by government officials who assume that everyone knows the technical difference between materials being *generated* (regrettably termed "*waste* stream") and waste being sent on for disposal. *They don't!* And too often the media jump to an easy but false conclusion that waste generation or the *waste stream* simply means "waste disposal." *It doesn't.*

Here's an illustration of what can happen, based on a real case. A pie chart in a government document is titled "Waste Stream." It doesn't define what *waste stream* means, and it doesn't break down the components of that waste stream in any great detail. But from other publicly available data, it can be deduced that a portion of that waste stream includes some 170,000 tonnes of corrugated boxes coming from households.

It's not surprising, then, that some media and consumers would immediately jump to the conclusion that 170,000 tonnes of corrugated boxes ended up in landfill (as part of the waste stream). *I mean, why is it called waste if it doesn't end up in landfill!*

The facts of the case tell a completely different story. While it is true that 170,000 tonnes of corrugated boxes were generated (that is, available for something to happen to them after use), it is certainly not true that all of those corrugated boxes ended up in landfill. In fact, in this case, some 92% of them were sent on for recycling. You can see the huge difference in public perception between 100% going to the dump (the 170,000 tonnes) and finding out that, in fact, only 8% did![1]

Here are two fictional headlines showing how a different story can be told. And both headlines are technically accurate!

See also **WASTE (DEFINITIONS)**.

Chapter 12

Google
Needs to clean up its image

I am going to ask you to do something that no self-respecting writer should ever do. And that's to momentarily take your eyes off these wonderfully crafted words and do a Google search. I am so sure of your loyalty that I know you'll come back. See, you're still reading!

Okay, here's what I want you to do. Go to Google and use the search terms *"images of deforestation in the United States"* or *"images of deforestation in Canada."* I guarantee that you will see something like this.

You're still reading, aren't you? You'll find pages and pages of visual images of mostly clear-cut forest. Some very ugly scenes. Definitely not feel-good pictures. Now, before I have to send out a search party for you, come back here. Because what you have seen with your very own eyes is a hugely effective promotion of a big fat lie. The big fat lie is that forestry is the major cause of deforestation in North America.

Yes, there are images of trees that have been felled. And yes, they don't look particularly nice. Neither do trees that have been devastated by insects or ravaged by fire. *But it's what you don't see here that's important.*

Because these are not necessarily images of deforestation. *I kid you not.* These are images of forest being cleared, yes. But as has been pointed out elsewhere in this book, deforestation is *far more than just forest being cleared*. Deforestation includes the conversion of that forest land into non-forest uses such as agriculture, oil and gas projects, hydro reservoirs, and residential subdivisions. Deforested land is forest land that's basically gone for good. It's not coming back to forest.

And the major cause of that deforestation in North America is not the forest industry, it's the conversion of forest land to agriculture. So, the images of deforestation that Google *should* be showing to depict deforestation in North America are images not of forest after it has been harvested (and before it's regrown) but images of *what deforestation truly is*: a deforested field of farmer's hay, of gently waving corn, of oil and gas exploration, of a mining quarry, a hydro-electric reservoir, of residential subdivisions, of ski hills and golf courses.

These are the *real images, the real face of deforestation* in North America. So why doesn't Google (or the other search engines, for that matter) show the images of what deforestation really means?

I put the case to Google. This is how it replied:

Yes, a big fat nothing response! I will keep you updated if and when I hear something.

GOOGLE | 57

Chapter 13

Hundred (100%) Fully, Completely
Nothing is 100% Recyclable or 100% Compostable!

While most of us never scored 100% on high school math tests, we know very well that 100% is the very best. Which is why it is so attractive to sales and marketing types when making environmental claims. What could be better than 100%? Nothing. The same goes for *fully* and *completely*. To consumers, this means 100%.

The most frequent claim consumers see is probably "100% Recyclable" and "100% Compostable." The 100% claim is also promoted as something of a *collective* target by stakeholder groups, and proudly announced in some government declarations. Are these claims accurate? Are they legal? Or are they just another form of greenwash?

100% Recyclable

100% Recyclable and 100% Compostable:
To most people, *recyclable* means "able to be recycled" and *compostable* means "able to be composted." Throw the 100% in front, and it would be

reasonable to assume that all of a product or package is able to be recycled or all of it is able to be composted.

Achieving this desirable state, however, requires meeting two conditions. The first is that there is no waste, that absolutely 100% of the material or materials can be recycled or composted. And the second is that there must be a way for consumers to actually do it. The first is a *technical* condition, the second is more of a *logistical* condition. But both must be met. Because this is an *environmental* claim, not a simple statement that 100% of something is *technically* capable of being recycled or composted.

And the Federal Trade Commission in the United States and the Competition Bureau in Canada clearly tie recyclable and compostable claims to the geography of the marketplace being served and the availability of an established recycling or composting program, and not to whether a material is simply *technically* capable of being recycled or composted.

Unfortunately, however, both the US *Green Guides* and the Canadian Competition Bureau are totally silent on 100% claims. The *Green Guides* clearly state: "A product should not be marketed as recyclable *unless it can be collected, separated, or otherwise recovered from the waste stream through an established recycling program* (emphasis added)."[1] In other words, the use of the recyclable claim is *directly connected* to the consumer's ability to access a recycling program. The *Guides* go on to outline how marketers need to qualify recyclable claims depending on the level of that access.

In a Competition Bureau publication, Canada too, states that claiming a product is recyclable *always* depends on the existence of (recycling) systems or facilities, adding that *"systems or facilities must be conveniently available to a reasonable proportion of purchasers, potential purchasers, and users in the area that the product is to be sold; otherwise, such claims could be considered false or misleading* (emphasis added)."[2]

Both these guidelines refer to recyclable and compostable claims in general. In the case of composting, marketers must further clarify whether the composting claim applies to at-home composting or to a municipal or industry composting program. But both government bodies connect the claim to access: to being able to place an item in a recycling or composting program.

And what if those programs are not available to everyone (which is what 100% implies)? There are remote communities in both countries that will likely *never* have "conveniently available" access to such programs. *So why are these claims allowed?* They give consumers the impression that 100% of these products or packages can be recycled or composted by everyone. *Is that true?*

To my mind, anyone placing 100% in front of recyclable or compostable is failing to follow the United States and Canadian guidelines and is leaving themselves open to prosecution for misleading advertising. They are compounding existing consumer confusion, or worse, deliberately indulging in what amounts to greenwashing, giving the impression that not only is their product 100% recyclable or compostable (technically) but that it can also be recycled or composted *everywhere*.

This is not true. Both technical and logistical conditions for making the environmental claim should be met. The product should be both *technically* recyclable/compostable and *able to be recycled/composted*. It's not one or the other. It's both.

I put this point of view to Canada's Competition Bureau. I received the standard reply about the relevant acts of Parliament et cetera and the role of the Bureau, and was told that my concerns had been referred to an officer for review. That was in back in June. In August, I received an update: "The Bureau continues to work in this area and will provide you with a more fulsome response at a later date."

Well, I am glad that someone is working on it, but I think it's long past time when we need clarification of 100% claims because there seem to be more and more of them every day and more and more confusion about what they mean, if anything.

100% Reusable, Recyclable, or Recoverable

What does "100% reusable, recyclable, or, where viable alternatives do not exist, recoverable" mean? These are the words in the Ocean Plastic Charter that Canada signed along with other G7 countries, except Japan and the United States. But what do they actually mean?[3]

The use of 100% implies *everything*, right? So, there will be no plastic waste? Well, not exactly. The Canadian Council of Ministers for the Environment (CCME) has since clarified that the 100% is an ideal and that zero-waste is just a target. It does not mean zero plastic.[4]

What about *reusable*? Does it mean "forever"? What happens when a reusable container can't be reused anymore? Can it now be thrown in landfill because at some time it was reused and still be counted in the calculation of a diversion rate?

And what does *recoverable* mean? Does it mean "energy recovery" or just "able to be recovered"? Most everything's able to be recovered right now. We are just not physically recovering it all! It seems that the CCME may now have drawn a line: *recovery* apparently means "everything other than dumping something in landfill or burning it without energy recovery." [5]

Given the lack of harmonization of definitions and methodologies it's going to be rather interesting to see how progress towards this 100% "ideal" will be measured (let alone achieved). It certainly *sounds* impressive.

I get the distinct impression that some of the packaged goods companies jumping on the bandwagon and saying they will reach such-and-such a goal by such-and-such a date don't totally understand what they are promising. And when they find out that a certain goal was never feasible with a certain material in the first place, or never achievable because of geographic constraints, they're going to have a lot of egg on their faces. And be accused of greenwashing. Governments too.

One senior executive I spoke to recently suggested that intentional or accidental greenwashing by large corporations had actually diminished in recent years, maybe because companies now had more environmental or sustainability specialists on staff, or available to them; that what were once lower-level and somewhat impractical environmental plans had now become more savvy and aggressive corporate goals or part of an environmental, social and governance (ESG) strategy. He also noted that social media criticism had become a far more effective (if a somewhat misguided) watchdog on both company claims and performance.

See also **RECYCLABLE** and **RECYCLED versus RECYCLABLE.**

Chapter 14

Hypocrisy?
These folks have some explaining to do

1. Heather Reisman

In an excerpt from her recent book, Indigo Books and Music CEO Heather Reisman calls modern paper use "wildly unsustainable" and criticizes the "clearcutting (of) centuries-old forests." Setting aside the inaccuracy of the "centuries-old" claim (see **"ANCIENT" FORESTS**), Reisman's own home and every Indigo bookstore probably exist because of a clear-cut, and as a seller of books printed on paper for many years one would expect her to have made a pretty penny on them. A case of believe what I say, not what I do?[1]

2. The Natural Resources Defense Council (NRDC) and STAND.earth

These environmental advocacy groups are harshly critical of clear-cutting forests, claiming in a recent report that "clearcutting decimates the ecosystem."[2] So why are they supporting and promoting the Forest Stewardship Council (FSC) whose standards allow clear-cutting; that recognizes that clear-cutting in a natural pattern with residuals emulates natural disturbances of the forest?[3]

In fact, STAND.earth (which used to be called ForestEthics) was very supportive when a new clear-cutting technique called natural range of variation (NRV) was introduced in 2016. This clear-cutting harvesting pattern mimics the natural disturbance rhythms of the forest (fire, wind, and pests) and is currently being implemented across the Canadian boreal forest.

In a press release introducing this new clear-cutting technique, the executive director of ForestEthics, Todd Paglia, was quoted as saying his organization was "pleased to see steps being taken towards timber harvesting that more closely mimic nature."[4] But clear-cutting still "decimates the ecosystem?"

LOGGING
Clearcutting decimates the ecosystem

NRDC/STAND.earth, The issue with Tissue, February 2019.

"... we are pleased to see steps being taken towards timber harvesting that more closely mimic nature."

Todd Paglia, Executive Director of ForestEthics, 2016.

3. Provinces and states promoting the circular economy

Numerous provinces and states are promoting a break from what's called the traditional linear economy of take-make-waste in favour of a circular economy where waste and pollution are "designed out," products and materials are kept in use, and natural systems are regenerated.

But those same provinces and states are doing little or nothing to change the economics that currently make it cheaper to send stuff to landfill rather than to recycle it. Some of the policy tools available include disposal bans or landfill surcharges on certain materials for which there are end-markets. Maybe it's time for those provinces and states to do something they have some control over, rather than telling other people what to do all the time?

4. Canopy and the burning of trash

The Vancouver-based environmental group Canopy promotes paper made from wheat straw by stating that leftover straw no longer has to be burned in the field just to get rid of it, creating air pollution and so on.

But Canopy also promotes sugarcane (bagasse) as an alternative to paper fibre. Part of the bagasse life cycle is the unpleasant environmental impact of burning trash in the sugar-cane fields. Canopy wants to avoid burning trash by promoting wheat straw, but is okay with burning trash to promote bagasse? See **SUGARCANE (BAGASSE)**. You can't have it both ways!

5. Banks and credit card companies

How's this for hypocrisy? On the one hand, banks are urging customers to "go green, go paperless" or "go paperless, save trees." At the same time, they're bombarding consumers with credit card application forms in the mail (paper and envelopes). Sort of undercuts their argument a bit, don't you think? See "**PAPERLESS.**"

6. Paper is bad, but then it's good

Eco Kloud advertises its sugarcane (bagasse) line of products as being environmentally superior to Styrofoam, plastic, and paper ("cutting trees"). Then it claims its paper soup bowls are a "much better alternative to Styrofoam (non-degradable) and plastic (non-biodegradable, petroleum based, pollutants)"and that its paper hot cups are "better alternatives to Styrofoam." Whatever happened to the "cutting trees" part? I guess the cup and bowl stock is tree paper.[5]

Chapter 15

"Killing" And "Saving" Trees
What exactly does this mean?

To be human, it seems, is to be a hypocrite. We kill trees all the time, and have done so for thousands of years. Same with fish, chickens, goats, sheep, cows - you name it. Sure, we may call it *harvesting* or *farming* or some less emotional word than *killing*, but the end result is the same: we regularly kill other animals or living things to make our lives more comfortable.

We are rather delicate beings, though. There's no way most of us will sever a chicken's head or slash a goat's throat - or murder a cow so we can enjoy a hamburger. We need *other* people to do that, preferably out-of-sight and out-of-mind. We don't want to think about it. We just want our chicken, goat, or hamburger, and as soon as possible please.

It's the same with trees and the products of trees. If we think about them at all (and mostly we don't), trees provide us with the basic necessities of life: shelter, fire, and food. There are other, perhaps less obvious benefits such as reducing air pollution, preventing soil erosion, improving water quality by filtering out impurities, and providing a protective canopy for other plant and animal species to grow and flourish.[1] And yes, they make us happy too![2] More importantly, however, trees act as one of the "lungs" of the Earth, sucking in carbon dioxide and expelling oxygen. Without oxygen, we would not survive.

So, collectively we have a vested interest in preserving and maintaining a vibrant, sustainable, diverse, and renewable resource at the very same time that we are "killing" it. The debate is where and how we strike a balance between the two, and why the emotional *killing* word is front and centre, joining the family of killing and saving whales, seals, Siberian tigers, polar bears, and so on. Each is portrayed as endangered and in need of rescue, and the emotional rally cry is the result. In the heat of the campaign, the facts often get mislaid, lost, distorted, obscured.

So, let's accept the fact that we kill/harvest/farm trees for lumber and paper products. The real questions are: Which trees? How many of them? How do we kill them? And how do we replace them? And there are strong views on all sides of those questions.

How we "kill" trees

The most common image of "killing" trees, of course, is the ugly clear-cut.[3] This is used by environmental groups and competitors to the lumber and paper industries to portray forestry in a bad light and to convince people that there is a better way (a better way to harvest trees or not to harvest them at all, or "better" alternatives such as steel, cement, plastic, or even wheat straw).

Foresters will tell you, however, that the clear-cutting method of harvesting mimics some of the natural disturbance dynamics of the forest, such as fire, wind blow-downs, and insect infestations. These don't look so pretty either! According to the World Resources Institute and the World Business Council for Sustainable Development, clear-cutting "allows regeneration and rapid growth of certain tree species" in some eco-systems. "It costs less, making forests more economically viable; (and) it produces safer working conditions for loggers."[4]

Clear-cutting provides the full sunlight that's needed for native pioneer species such as jack pine and aspen to regenerate naturally in Canada's boreal forests. And the size and distribution of clear-cuts is determined by looking at past natural disturbance patterns. Streams, rivers, lakes, and wetlands are protected by the creation of reserves within the harvested area, retaining natural variations and biodiversity.[5]

A group of Canadian forest companies and leading environmental groups recently committed to move towards implementing a new clear-cutting harvesting technique called *natural range of variation* (NRV). It mimics the natural disturbance dynamics of the forest (fire, wind, and pests) and is currently being implemented across the boreal.

In a press release at the time, environmental group ForestEthics (now STAND.earth) was supportive, saying it was "pleased to see steps being taken towards timber harvesting that more closely mimic nature."[6] Despite its poor public image, then, clear-cutting is not the evil that some people portray it to be (see **HYPOCRISY?**).

Which trees, and how many?

A key issue for the forest industry, landowners, governments, scientists, and environmental groups is which trees get to be harvested, and how many. These decisions are always site-specific, but the broad parameters include consideration of the ages of the trees, the species involved, the wood volume available, and the sustainable limit of the area to be logged[7] (see "OLD-GROWTH" FORESTS).

Here we get into arguments about which forest areas and how much of them should forever be off-limits to logging and other extractive industries; how much needs to be protected and preserved to retain biodiversity; the implications for wildlife; what the carbon consequences of harvesting the forest are; and even debates about what the trees are used for (see **TOILET PAPER**).

This is all good and healthy. We should be open to debate. In Canada, unlike the United States where private ownership of forest is dominant, more than 90% of Canada's forests are on publicly owned land.[8] This has enabled governments to introduce extensive rules and regulations about what logging companies can and cannot do, all framed around the policy of sustainable forest management.[9]

Any forest area harvested, for example, must be successfully regenerated either naturally or artificially (through tree planting or seeding) after harvest, a fact that some activists conveniently neglect to mention when denouncing how many millions or billions of trees are being removed (see **OMISSIONS** and "**TREE-FREE**").

Canada was an early adopter of sustainable forest management and together with the United States and 10 other countries established what became known internationally as the Montreal Process whereby "a common set of science-based indicators (gives) government, industry, researchers and the public, a way to consistently define, assess, monitor and report progress on the sustainable management of 90% of the world's boreal and temperate forests."[10] These sustainability indicators have been modified

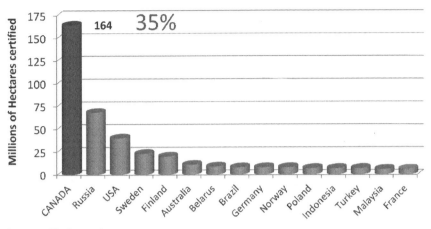

Source: certificationcanada.org

over the years and are designed to be comparable to those of other countries, and to be consistent with global forest reporting to the United Nations.[11]

Independent third-party certification of sustainably managed forests is an important yardstick. And Canada can take some pride in the fact that more of its forest is independently certified than anywhere else in the world. A whopping 35% of the entire world's certified forest is in Canada.[12]

So, what about "saving" trees?

The problem here is that *saving* can be interpreted in so many different ways. First up, of course, is that we are not really saving trees (from death) if they are eventually going to die anyway. Saving, in effect, is really just postponing the inevitable.

Second, there is evidence to suggest that the notion of "saving paper to save trees" is fundamentally flawed. Dr. Jim Bowyer and his colleagues at Dovetail Partners have tracked recent cases and trends where paper production was reduced:[13]

- In the Southern United States, there has been a significant decline in paper consumption over the past two decades, especially in printing and writing paper, because of the shift to electronic formats; the 2007-2009 recession; and stiffer competition from Asia. Mill closures and lost capacity followed. Forest landowners (mostly individuals and families, investment groups, and forest companies) responded to the market signals and considered their options: convert the forest to agriculture because of higher commodity prices to be received there (deforestation); use the wood to produce pellets for energy production; or remove the forest for vacation homes or other urban development (deforestation again).

> Let's accept the fact that we kill/harvest/farm trees for lumber and paper products. The real questions are: Which trees? How many of them? How do we kill them? And how do we replace them? And there are strong views on all sides of those questions.

- In northern New Brunswick, three large pulp mills closed over the past decade. But this has not meant fewer trees cut. Sawmills are accepting lower diameter logs (which would have gone to pulp); trees are being harvested for other purposes (mills in Atholville and Nackawic have been converted to make dissolving pulp, which is used to produce viscose rayon for the textile market in India); and logs are being used to manufacture oriented strand board and to supply a growing pellets-for-energy market.
- In Minnesota, the recent closure of several mills led to large blocks of forest land being divested. Several thousand acres of this land was subsequently cleared and converted to intensive agriculture, including potato production (deforestation).

Dr. Bowyer and his colleagues conclude that, counterintuitively, the continued use of paper and other wood products may, in fact, be an essential component in maintaining a forested landscape for future generations.

When it comes to saving trees or forest, much depends on what type of trees we are talking about, and where they are. If primary forest (forest basically untouched by humans so far) is the target, then it could be argued that those particular or specific forest areas are being saved by being protected. So here *saving* really means "protected," perhaps being declared legally off-limits or incorporated into a wilderness area.

But if it is forest that has already been logged (and has since been restocked), are you really saving any trees? Without an *operational* definition (not an *academic* one) of exactly what a primary forest is or is not, this debate will likely continue (see **FOREST**).

Then there are the marketing claims by competing industries. Are we really saving trees by using steel and cement as building materials?[14] Are we saving trees by using plastic shopping bags?[15] Are we saving trees by using sugarcane (bagasse)[16] or wheat straw? Corporations make unsubstantiated claims as well.[17] In each case, the alternative material might very well be worse for the environment.[18] We need life-cycle analyses that meet ISO 14040 standards, including publicly available independent third-party reviews, to help us with that. And in the meantime, the trees will still be growing, and dying.

We can certainly reduce how much wood and paper fibre we use when we extract it or convert it into a wood or paper product.[19] This makes economic sense because it saves on production costs and perhaps wins over a client from a competitor. Whether this amounts to saving trees or not is a moot point. It's certainly a marketing point.

With so many claims for saving trees from both customers and competitors, it was inevitable that the paper industry itself would get into the game. And when the sales and marketing types from the virgin mills claim paper from recycled mills is too weak compared to their sheet, it's not surprising that the recycled mills quickly point out how many trees the virgin mills are killing, or even more disingenuously, suggest that they (the recycled mills) don't kill *any* trees.[20]

And then there are the eco-calculators that massage all sorts of numbers from supposedly soundly based scientific assumptions, calculations, and formulas to come up with exactly how many trees are allegedly being "saved" by buying this or that. It's all a bit of a mess, really! Buyer beware!

See also **ENVIRONMENTALLY FRIENDLY, ECO-FRIENDLY; FOREST; HYPOCRISY?; "OLD-GROWTH" FORESTS; OMISSIONS; SUGARCANE (BAGASSE); "TREE-FREE;"** and **TOILET PAPER.**

Chapter 16

"Old-Growth" Forest
Has many meanings and is an emotional trigger

The problem with *old-growth* is that there are at least two broad (and differing) definitions of what it means.

1. When old growth is used to mean "primary" forest

To some people, *old growth* is all about how to retain the world's remaining *primary* forests, those forests comprising native species without clearly visible indications of human activity, and where ecological processes are not significantly disturbed. Used in this sense, *old growth* means forests that have had no, or minimal, contact with humans, or that have never been logged before or been impacted by fire suppression efforts.

These primary forests, they argue, should be left alone. And we are talking about complete forests here, regardless of the age of the trees: young, middle-aged, and old trees all together (so *old* is a bit of a misnomer).[1]

As noted in the **FOREST** entry, most (61%) of the world's remaining primary forest is in three countries (Brazil, Canada, and the United States). The United States is estimated to have 75 million hectares and Canada 205 million hectares. But bear in mind that the definition of primary forests is an *academic* one at this stage, rather than an *operational* one. Canada, for example, does not have any original data on primary forest. Any estimates are based on extrapolations from multiple data sets and methodologies.[2]

Here's the current overview:

Canada's Forest Lands: 346.9 million hectares[1]
  Naturally Regenerating Forest: 328.8 million hectares[2]
    Primary Forest (est): 205.1 million hectares[3]
  Other Naturally Regenerating Forest: 123.6 million hectares[4]
Planted Forest: 18.2 million hectares[5]
Annual Harvest (2018): 0.7 million hectares[6]

Unlike in the United States, where private ownership of forest land is dominant, forests in Canada are overwhelmingly (94%) owned by the public through provincial, territorial, and federal governments.[3] So, in Canada it is the provincial government foresters, ecologists, and wildlife biologists who determine how forest lands should be managed: whether they should be left in a wilderness state; set aside as parks; converted to pasture or crops; opened to oil and gas exploration, mining, or forestry; retained for recreation and tourism; or removed for the construction of hydro dams, roads, towns, subdivisions, ski hills or golf courses.

Some 11% of Canada's total forest land is already *legally protected* from development.[4] That's about the size of the United Kingdom, with industrial activities such as harvesting, mining, and hydro-electric development banned in nearly 95% of it.[5] The percentage of legally protected forest cover varies by province: from a high of 14% in Nova Scotia, British Columbia and Alberta down to 4%-6% in Yukon, Newfoundland and Labrador, Nunavut, New Brunswick, and Prince Edward Island.[6]

In addition to the 11% that's legally protected, there's a whopping 41% of Canada's forest cover that's left *unmanaged*.[7] Much of it is remote and inaccessible and left in a wilderness state, disturbed only by fire, insects and beetles, winds, floods, and avalanches. And more recently by a warming climate.

What remains (48%) is called *managed* forest: forest land under a forest

---

1 State of Canada's Forests Annual Report, 2020.
2 Canada's estimate for FRA 2020.
3 Ibid.
4 Ibid.
5 Ibid.
6 State of Canada's Forests Annual Report, 2020.

Canada's Forest Lands

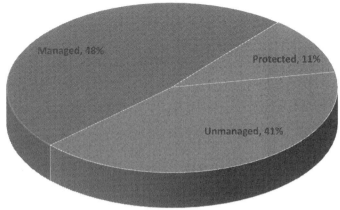

Source: FPAC, 2020

management plan using the science of forestry.[8] In deciding which areas will be available for harvesting, provincial foresters take into account the likely impact on the forest of natural disturbances such as insects, disease, and forest fires; the possible impact on wildlife and habitat; the wood volume available; the sustainable limit of the area to be logged; and various economic and social benefits such as local employment, recreation, and Indigenous land rights.

Foresters first identify the forest values they want to protect and then identify local biological conditions so that they can set limits and targets for different tree types and age classes. They use the growth rate of trees and their knowledge of tree science to establish what they consider to be a sustainable wood supply and also set aside areas of concern, sometimes called high-value conservation areas. A recent study indicated that over half of Canada's managed forest contains conservation areas within it (for example, riparian and woodland caribou management zones) where harvesting does not occur or is deferred. Which means, when you look at the big picture, that less than 25% of Canada's forest area is actually available for harvest.[9]

2. When "old growth" means "older trees"

A second definition of *old growth* centres on the actual age of the trees to be harvested, and not necessarily on whether the forest has been logged before. Should old-growth trees be left to die naturally, or should they be harvested so their declining carbon stock can be locked into wood products and not lost when they die? The focus here is specifically on the fate of older trees, rather than the whole forest per se.

First, a quick background on the three stages of the forest life cycle: young, middle-aged, and old. There is the young, open forest, such as seen after a natural disturbance like fire; the middle-aged forest with a dense canopy of trees after the weaker trees have been outgrown; and the old-growth forest of larger trees with a complex structure, including smaller trees, fallen logs, and other debris on the forest floor.[10] There is a natural selection at work here as the young replace the old: a life cycle of continuous renewal.

Okay, so how old is old? In Canada, the national forestry database classifies trees into 12 different age categories, with the top range being trees more than 200 years old. However, these worthy survivors represent only 4% of the total because, overall, Canada's trees are relatively young. In fact, most are less than 100 years old![11] (See the discussion in **"ANCIENT" FORESTS**).

These older trees are pretty much confined to two of Canada's 12 ecozones (the temperate rainforest of the British Columbia coast, and the Montane Cordillera which stretches from north-central BC southeast to the Alberta foothills and south to the US border). Together, these two ecozones, which represent just 12% of Canada's total forest lands, contain some 82% of Canada's oldest trees: mostly fir, hemlock, and spruce.[12] This geographic and climatic reality helps explain why old growth is such a hot issue in British Columbia.

Having older trees, however, doesn't necessarily mean old-growth trees. That's because trees live to different ages. Birch and maple trees, for example, have far shorter lives than fir and hemlock. So, it is *forest type* that more determines whether a tree is considered to be old-growth or not.

And the people who decide that in Canada are the provincial foresters. And this being Canada, the definition varies by province! More accurately, it differs by forest type. This is why British Columbia, for example, has two indices. According to the provincial government: "Most of BC's coastal forests are considered to be old growth if they contain trees that are more than 250 years old. Some types of interior forests are considered to be old growth if they contain trees that are more than 140 years old."[13]

The question of carbon

Then there's the carbon question. The release of carbon when a tree dies and the role of forests as carbon sinks and sources is a key discussion topic, especially today.

Talk to foresters and they will tell you that older and bigger trees in the boreal forest do store a lot of carbon although they don't sequester much. They are also more prone to fire, thus potentially dramatically reducing their ability to store carbon. By contrast, young trees in the boreal do not absorb much carbon. It's the middle-aged ones that are great at putting on the weight. Heard that one before?

In tropical forests, and possibly temperate rainforests, however, it is understood that old-growth trees store more carbon because the natural tree turnover is lower and the trees generally live much longer than in the boreal.

Another key factor is humidity. In a *wet* ecosystem, forests can continuously sequester carbon into a growing pool for hundreds of years. In a *fire-driven* ecosystem, however, carbon can be released on a frequent basis, which makes its storage in forest products more relevant.

"We often hear," said one forester, "that protecting forests has a positive climate impact because old-growth trees store and sequester vast amounts of carbon. Our typical response is that the absence of foresters and their management plans does not always mean a forest will become a carbon sink. Disturbance-prone forests are becoming carbon sources because of increasing rates of insect and beetle infestations and fire, in part due to climate change. While it's true that old-growth can be a significant carbon store, it's also true that in some areas these trees are increasingly turning from carbon sinks into carbon sources."

So, there you have it. Two starkly different definitions of *old-growth*: one focussed on retaining the world's remaining primary (never logged before) forest, and the other centred on determining what an old-growth tree actually is, and the consequences of harvesting it or leaving it alone.

While it is certainly possible to hold both these positions at the same time, it is very confusing when the same term (*old-growth*) is so broadly applied. Personally, I think *primary* should be used when talking about forest that has not been logged before, and *old-growth* only when talking specifically about the harvesting of older trees. To a non-forester like myself, this makes better sense, I think! We need to understand exactly what we are referring to!

Currently, when covering these contentious forestry issues, many journalists and bloggers tend to simply throw in the term *old-growth* without considering whether it is applicable or even what it means. Does *old growth* mean primary (never logged before) forest of whatever tree age? Or does it mean the older trees in a forest? There's a big difference. And I think this adds considerably to the public confusion (and emotion) on this issue.

So, the next time you hear or see the term *old-growth*, please recognize that there is no single widely accepted definition of it; that old-growth varies between forest types; and that the whole question of carbon (sinks versus stores) is wide open at this stage.

See also **"ANCIENT" FORESTS, FOREST**, and **"KILLING" AND "SAVING" TREES.**

Chapter 17

Omissions
Leaving information out can be as misleading as telling little green lies in the first place

(Some of these omissions are featured in more detail in other entries).

1. A feature on deforestation by the forest industry had no input from the forest industry!

In late 2019 the Toronto-based *Globe and Mail* newspaper ran an extensive two-page feature on a study claiming that logging scars in Ontario forests were large enough to account for "seven times the annual reported rate of deforestation in all provinces combined."[1]

There was no independent analysis of the statistical assumptions and methodologies used to come to this conclusion (which is suspect)[2] and no context was given for what causes deforestation in Canada or how it is measured (Ontario and Canada follow United Nations guidelines).[3]

What was particularly disturbing, though, was that the *only* people interviewed for the feature were all involved in the study in some way (one wrote it, another helped fund it, the third provided some "thoughtful guidance)."[4] And no, the *Globe* didn't tell readers that the cement industry helped fund the work.[5] In an 1100-word feature on deforestation by the forest industry there was no input from the forest industry! Only a letter to the editor published subsequently.

The big headlines with the word *deforestation* prominent, with no context provided, simply reinforced a false and very public impression of significant deforestation on the part of the forest industry. In fact, the industry's deforestation rate back then was a mere 0.0004% (yes, three zeroes and a four). Some 1,368 hectares out of 347 *million* hectares.[6] That's certainly not the impression readers would have got (see **DEFORESTATION** for more details). The latest data is:

Canada's Forest Lands: 346,962,664 hectares
Deforestation (all causes): 34,257 hectares (0.0098%)
Deforestation (forestry): 1,494 hectares (0.0004%)

2. Pulp fiction

In a blog entitled *"What's in the Box?"* Canadian environmental group Canopy answers its question with a bald-faced lie, giving the impression that paper boxes are mostly made from virgin market pulp.[7] This is not true. It is certainly not true in Canada. Very little virgin pulp is used by Canadian mills to make boxes in Canada.

Quite the contrary. Most are made from 100% recycled board[8] that's been collected from the back of Canadian factories and supermarkets, from offices, or from Blue Box programs and depots. The Paper & Paperboard Packaging Environmental Council (PPEC) pioneered the further recycling of old boxboard in North America way back in the 1990s. And almost every Canadian can put paper boxes out for recycling today.[9]

While it is true that some virgin pulp is exported from Canada, it mainly goes into the production of printing and writing, sanitary, and specialty papers. Only a small portion of it ends up in packaging products. So yes, it is both possible and likely that some of this exported pulp is shipped back to Canada as packaging with a product inside. But to imply that virgin pulp represents the prime component of the Canadian industry's feedstock for boxes, when most of it is 100% recycled content, is a gross distortion of fact. See *"Canopy makes more embarrassing 'boo-boos'"*[10]

3. Only one side of the story being told

It's easy to point to trees being cut down and to be critical of some of the uses to which that wood fibre is put. Fair enough. But to completely ignore the other side of the ledger, that new trees are planted to regenerate the forest that's been harvested, is dishonest. This is provincial law in Canada, where governments own more than 90% of the forest. Logged areas must be successfully regenerated after harvest, either naturally or artificially (through tree planting and seeding).

In Canada, this averages just less than 1,000 new seedlings a minute.[11] Some environmental advocates don't seem to care about this. All they are focused on is telling the public how many trees are allegedly cut down and mentioning absolutely nothing about the legal requirements (and the business sense) in regenerating the harvested area so that the forest resource is there for the future.

4. Where are the independent life cycle reviews?

The Vancouver-based environmental group Canopy has launched a campaign against paper packaging while touting wheat straw and other alternative fibres as "environmentally better." But so far Canopy's favourite mill (launched in 2018) has not produced for public review a life-cycle analysis that meets ISO 14040 standards.

Making life-cycle and carbon footprint claims in a nine-page slide presentation on its website doesn't say much except how great Columbia Pulp is, with no back-up information. How about a life-cycle analysis that meets ISO 14040 standards, including a publicly available independent third-party review (see "**TREE-FREE**")?

The same applies to the reusable tote scheme (Loop) being promoted by Terra Cycle to retailers. Where's the publicly available independent third-party review to back up all the environmental claims being made? We ain't seen nothing yet!

5. Is digital really better?

Banks and insurance companies have been quick to urge customers to "go green, go paperless" but not so quick to acknowledge the environmental impact of electronic communications: the energy required to run computers and send emails; through to the mining of rare earth and scarce metals; to the amount of e-waste that ends up in landfills (see "**PAPERLESS**").

6. What about the avoided costs?

It's popular in media circles these days to proclaim that "Recycling is dead." Few of these advocates consider the alternatives, and the avoided costs of *not* recycling: *more* extraction of resources and energy; *more* landfills; and *more* methane and carbon dioxide emissions (see **RECYCLING**).

7. Difficult to recycle materials that end up in landfill

Of course, some materials do. But just because they are challenging doesn't make them unrecyclable. Cereal and shoe boxes (commonly called boxboard) have been recycled in Canada since the 1990s. In fact, 94% of Canadians can recycle them today. The rest can be composted. Soiled pizza boxes are not a problem either. And milk cartons are also recyclable in a mill that has the special equipment (a hydrapulper) to do so (see **PIZZA BOXES** and **RECYCLED**).

8. Being recyclable doesn't mean it was actually recycled

The *recyclable* word or logo on a product or package means that the product material is technically recyclable and that enough consumers in the area can actually put it out to the curb for recycling. *But that's just the beginning of the journey.* And there are no guarantees that the material will actually end up in a new product (see **RECOVERY AND RECYCLING RATES, RECYCLED, RECYCLED versus RECYCLABLE, RECYCLING,** and **RECYCLABLE**).

9. It's all that packaging, clogging our landfills!

Well, actually it's not. Sure, a lot of packaging (far too much) does end up in landfill, but it's by no means the major stuff we are collectively trashing. Packaging represents about 20% of what households send to landfill. That means there's another 80% out there that we need to pay far more attention to (see **PACKAGING WASTE**).

10. Environmental groups strangely silent when it suits them

A recent survey[12] of the websites and Facebook pages of 17 Canadian environmental groups known to have an interest in forestry issues showed that they had links to deforestation occurring elsewhere in the world plus a few Canadian examples. But not one of them mentioned the fact that Canada's deforestation rate was amongst the lowest in the world (0.01%).[13]

Only two websites mentioned the conversion of forest land to agriculture as a cause of deforestation, and then only generally in a list of causes. In fact, the conversion of forest land to agriculture was then, and still is, a major cause of deforestation in Canada. But there were no images of deforestation via agriculture on any of the Facebook pages and websites, even though nine times more forest was then permanently removed by farmers than by the frequently vilified forest and paper industries (see **DEFORESTATION**).

Chapter 18

Packaging Waste
Packaging is the villain again (sigh)

There is no doubt that some goods are over-packaged and that a lot more can be done to reduce the amount of paper, plastic, glass, and metal packaging that ends up in consumers' homes. Today, there's also an increased focus on single-use packaging, on reusable packaging, and on the impact of plastics on marine and human life.

But blaming packaging is only part of the story. To put it bluntly, we in the so-called developed world eat, drink, and buy far too much unnecessary *stuff*. And we're hooked on convenience, especially when it comes to food.

Consumption is the real issue, not the packaging that delivers it. As consumers, however, we struggle to limit how much we buy. It's so much easier to point the finger at the packaging that's left behind rather than at the product we bought. We *wanted* to buy the product at the time. The packaging just came with it, and now it's a nuisance.

But *before* that, the packaging delivered the product safely so that we could use or consume it. Few of us, for example, would even consider carrying a dozen eggs loose in our hands from the local store. Instead, it's far easier to buy a carton moulded to the shape of 12 eggs so that your hands are free to carry the carton along with the other items you bought at the same time. It was packaging that provided that safe, easy, and efficient option.

And depending on what you've bought and where it's coming from, packaging has to protect the product through a variety of distribution logistics (ships, planes, trains, trucks) and climate conditions (various temperatures and humidity levels), all while keeping the product undamaged, and, if it's food, fresh for as long as it typically takes to consume. And the packaging has to do all of these tasks economically, at a price the product will still sell at. And, of course, be reusable or recyclable afterwards.

Above: Beauty and toiletry and cosmetic packaging frequently draws criticism for being excessively packaged.

Thus, striking a balance between *over*-packaging and *under*-packaging is both extremely important and far more complicated than it seems at first sight.[1] We all know that *under*-packaging leads to damaged goods, which in turn means they have to be sent back to the manufacturer, adding to the product's cost, and to both the packaging and the product's overall environmental burden. There have been occasional reports of retailers simply dumping damaged goods to avoid such return costs, which is clearly not a good outcome either.

But it's the *waste* of packaging that gets most of the attention, even

PACKAGING WASTE | 83

though packaging represents only a small portion of the overall environmental burden of delivering a product to market.² What do we do with all this? Packaging is a soft political target. It's much easier for politicians to jump up and down about packaging than it is to confront consumers (who happen to be voters as well) with why they bought too much product in the first place, or why they tossed it in the garbage instead of sending it on for recycling.

I remember a provincial minister of the environment standing up at a recycling conference to complain at length about all the packaging that his new plasma TV had arrived in. Plasma was then all the rage. He didn't bother to explain *why* he needed a new TV, or what he was going to do with the old one. He just complained about all the packaging that had (safely) delivered his new one.

And then there are the gross exaggerations such as "our waste streams are clogged with unnecessary packaging at every turn." Sure, we can have a lively debate about what is *necessary* and what is not, but "clogging our waste streams at every turn" depends entirely on how much of the waste stream you measure.

In the most comprehensive national survey of packaging ever done in Canada, packaging represented only 13% of total solid waste disposed.³ While 13% is significant, it's not exactly *clogging*. This survey was conducted by Statistics Canada for the Canadian Council of Ministers for the Environment (CCME) and is now more than 20 years old, but there's no obvious reason why the percentage would be hugely different today.

If you really *wanted* to make packaging seem like a bigger problem, though, all you have to do is change what you measure. For example, if you remove sewage and sewage sludge, hazardous waste, and construction and demolition waste from the equation, then wow! the packaging portion suddenly climbs to 20%.⁴ Just like that, packaging's a big problem!

I am not saying that we should focus less attention on diverting packaging from landfill. Absolutely not. I *am* saying that maybe we should be paying *more* attention to other significant parts of the waste stream as well: in particular, to organics and construction, renovation and demolition debris. Household packaging, after all, is only between 10% and 17% of what residents put in the trash, depending on whose figures you believe.⁵

Put another way, some 80% of what we householders end up trashing is *not* packaging!

Unlike Canada, which has not updated any national packaging statistics since 1996, the United States regularly measures a waste category it calls "Containers and Packaging." But because the US Environmental Protection Agency (EPA) does not include all industrial or construction and demolition waste in its estimates, the packaging data in the US EPA model are unfortunately not directly comparable to those of its northern neighbour. Its latest report estimates containers and packaging disposal at 21% of municipal solid waste.[6]

Packaging 21% of municipal solid waste disposal in the United States

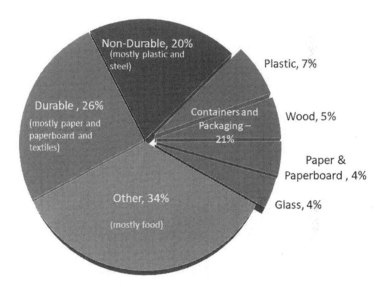

This simple example of differing ways of measuring solid waste highlights one of the major problems we face in making reasonable and credible comparisons on many waste issues, not just packaging, both nationally and internationally. For more background, see **WASTE (DEFINITIONS)**.

Chapter 19

"Paperless"
Is digital really better?

The Canadian and US guidelines for environmental marketing are very clear: comparative claims must be accurate and not misleading, and be backed up by research that meets recognized standards.[1] Claims like "go green, go paperless" and "go paperless, save trees" obviously do not meet these guidelines.

When did you ever see a bank or an insurance company or some other service provider offer an explanatory statement for claims like these? Did you ever see a description of the methods used to make the comparisons? Or results from a published standard or recognized test method? Have you ever seen the assumptions behind these comparative assertions? Because that's what those US and Canadian government guidelines suggest is necessary. "Go green, go paperless" and "go paperless, save trees" are nothing but nasty smears.

Not only do they denigrate a competitor (in this case, paper),[2] but they also completely fail to acknowledge the environmental impact of electronic communications. Because there is one, and it's considerable, stretching from the energy required to run computers and send emails[3] through to the mining of rare earth and scarce metals[4] to the amount of e-waste that ends up in landfills.[5]

The paper industry trade group Two Sides North America has been fighting this battle for several years, with some success. It says that more than 145 leading North American companies (including many in the Fortune 500) and over 700 companies globally have removed or corrected these false and misleading environmental claims. And it points to surveys indicating that many consumers see right through them.[6]

Between 58% and 61% of respondents in a recent survey of US and

Canadian consumers, for example, agreed that claims about the switch to digital being "better for the environment" were made because the sender wanted to save money.[7] A similar number of respondents argued that digital wasn't paperless anyway because they regularly had to print out documents at home if they wanted a hard copy. And almost all (90%) agreed that they should have the right to choose how they received communications (printed or electronic).[8]

It's clear that this battle and the trade-off between the two is far from over. But let's get the facts out on the table. *All the facts. Not just the smears and the greenwash.*

See also **"KILLING" AND "SAVING" TREES**.

Chapter 20

Pizza Boxes
What is it about pizza boxes?

I love pizza. Scoffing down all that cheese and pepperoni. Tearing into that soft fresh crust, knowing full well that my long-delayed and somewhat erratic weight loss program will be pushed back a few days, maybe weeks. Especially if that piping-hot and mushy mess is washed down with large dollops of ice cream. To cool it off, you understand.

But it's the box that the pizza comes in that I want to focus on here. Municipalities seem to go out of their way to make an example of the poor old pizza box. It's not recyclable, they claim. The paper mills don't want it. It's the mountains of grease and cheese. Put it in your organics or food waste bin. At least it will make good compost.

There is some truth to that. Paper can be composted, and for some households, composting is likely the better option. Ask the residents of Nova Scotia and Prince Edward Island, or any community that's hundreds of kilometres or miles from the nearest packaging recycling mill.

But pizza boxes are perfectly recyclable too. Sure, the recycling mills don't want the plastic centrepiece that stops the steaming contents from touching the lid and messing up the anchovies or pineapple slices. And they'd really prefer that you deal with your leftover crusts yourself. It's a pride thing.

But the box itself is fine. Normally it's made of corrugated board. And in Canada anyway, it's mostly 100% recycled content. So, it's been around before. And will be around again. What? you say. That gooey, greasy stuff from my last box will be in my next box too? *Yuck!*

No, dear friend, it won't. When it finally gets to a recycling mill, your pizza box is first dumped into a big washing machine called a pulper. Any crust you've mistakenly donated will be shaken free and exit the system. Same for the cheese. It tends to clump together and gets screened out during the pulping process.

Aha, but what about the grease? Well, that's a little harder to get rid of, but if you thought the pizza was hot, wait until you hear the temperatures that paper is made at. In a typical mill recycling process, the temperature of the paper sheet reaches 220 to 240 degrees Fahrenheit, well above 100 degrees Celsius, the boiling point of water and the temperature required for sterilization. So goodbye, grease! The average grease content of a pizza box is less than 2% anyway, which doesn't affect the strength of the new board being made.[1]

And if you still aren't totally convinced, there's a further check in the system. The board goes from the mill to a converting plant, where the board is blended with other paper layers to form a corrugated sheet, which will then be shaped into your next pizza box. The corrugation process destroys any bacteria that might remain. In fact, a recent study showed that every single one of 720 corrugated boxes from six different suppliers tested at six different locations in three different regions met acceptable sanitization levels.[2]

So, there you have it. Pizza boxes are recyclable. Now was that vegetarian or Hawaiian you wanted?

Chapter 21

Pristine And Undisturbed Forest

There is no such thing as an undisturbed forest

As a long-time hiker who appreciates forests, I can understand why people would want to describe some of them as pristine and undisturbed, unspoiled and unsullied, unpolluted and untouched. It's a no-brainer that we would want to protect them from too much (or, in some cases, *any*) human intrusion. I get that.

We are fooling ourselves, however, if we don't recognize that Nature herself is both beautiful and savage at the same time. Forest ecosystems are dynamic and constantly evolving, a complex array of plants, organisms, and microorganisms that interact both with themselves and their surroundings -- and have done so for thousands of years.

It is a little arrogant of us, then, to portray remote forest areas where humans, as far as we know, have not yet ventured in great numbers, as "pristine and undisturbed." Because Nature has been, and is there 24/7. For example, beetles, insects, and wildfires either damaged, infected, killed, or burned more than 18 million hectares of Canada's forest lands in 2018 with little or no assistance from humans. (That's an area 24 times larger than was logged for lumber and pulp and paper and regenerated afterwards).[1] And this happens year after year: a natural cycle of death and renewal. Let's not forget that Nature exists in all her beauty and savagery whether humans are around or not.

See also **"ANCIENT" FORESTS, BOREAL FOREST, DEFORESTATION, "DEGRADED" FOREST, and "OLD GROWTH" FOREST.**

Temporary Forest Disturbances

- Harvest: 4%
- Forest fires: 10%
- Insects and beetles: 86%

Source: State of Canada's Forests Annual Report, 2020

"Wood-boring beetles quickly colonise newly burned trees. Woodpeckers soon follow, feeding on the beetle larvae under the bark. Light-loving blueberries emerge after fire, with bumper crops providing essential nutrition for black bears and other animals. Jack pine relies on environmental triggers like the heat from fire to release seeds sealed inside its cones by sticky resin."

Excerpt from the State of Canada's Forests, Annual Report, 2017.

Chapter 22

"Recoverable"
Does this mean anything?

In a dictionary sense, *recoverable* means "able to be recovered, regained or retrieved, to be saved from loss and restored to usefulness." Its opposite is *irrecoverable* or *unrecoverable*, which means "incapable of being recovered or regained."

Most materials are physically recoverable, meaning we can physically recover them if we are willing to spend enough money to do so. For example, most paper products in North America are recoverable. Whether it makes economic sense to recover them from the remotest of communities is an entirely different question. And only parts of them may be useful in the same manufacturing process that created them in the first place because of contamination issues. But they are *recoverable*.[1]

So, when consumer packaged goods companies and governments put out press releases stating that their own specific packaging or that all packaging will be recoverable by such-and-such a date, they are not really promising much. Most packaging is recoverable now. *Whether it is actually being recovered, how it will be reused, and how much of it will be re-used or recycled, are the questions that we really need answers to.*

Chapter 23

Recovery And Recycling Rates

Ambiguity and confusion
open the door to little green lies

Do you know the difference between a waste diversion rate, a recovery rate, and a recycling rate? No? Join the crowd.

Perhaps the easiest way to explain it is to think big picture first, then narrow it down. And the big picture is *resource recovery* in general. When the word *recovery* is used in this broad sense, as in a government's resource recovery strategy, its meaning is relatively clear.

Resource recovery is a wide-ranging, all-encompassing strategy involving different material streams such as paper, plastic, glass, metals, organics, end-of-life vehicles, batteries, and electrical and electronic equipment, and so on; as well as different waste management options (reuse, recycling, composting, and the recovery of waste for conversion into alternative fuels or energy-from-waste plants).

As such, *recovery* is something of a favourite word in many international, government, and company position statements. It's broad, with enough wriggle room. For example, the G7 Ocean Plastics Charter has set itself the grand target of "100% reusable, recyclable, or, where viable alternatives do not exist, recoverable" materials. Quite helpfully, the charter doesn't define what any of this actually means, especially the *recoverable* part! Although in subsequent documents it apparently means everything other than dumping plastics in landfill or burning it without energy recovery.[1]

Waste diversion is also a broad strategy involving similar material streams and some of the same waste management options (recycling and composting). But there is a significant difference, as outlined in the widely accepted waste management hierarchy of preferred environmental options.

As the diagram over the page illustrates, the waste management hierarchy is divided into three broad areas: diversion, recovery, and disposal.

Waste Management Hierarchy

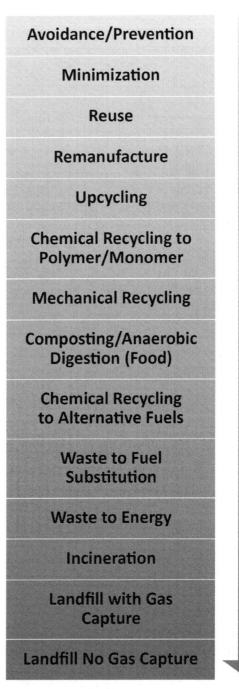

While there is ongoing debate about which particular waste strategy belongs where, and how these options should be interpreted, it is fair to say that the current consensus, at least at the government policy level, is that *recovery* options such as waste used for alternative fuels, fuel substitution, and in energy-from-waste plants are not considered to be diversion.

Although, without getting into the weeds here, it all depends on whether the jurisdiction is talking about diversion from landfill or diversion back into, for lack of a better phrase, a more circular economy. However, a *waste diversion rate* usually involves materials that are sent for recycling or composting, and not those sent on to energy-from-waste (EFW) plants.

The use of the word *recovery* (both in the broad resource recovery sense, and in the more specific energy-from-waste sense) has, and does, create some confusion. For this and other reasons, the European Union (EU) for years had two distinct waste targets: one for materials sent for mechanical *recycling* (paper, plastic, glass, and metal) and one for *recovery* of materials in EFW, gasification, or pyrolysis plants.[2]

Double meaning

The double meaning of the word *recovery* means it is crucial to compare apples with apples as much as possible. As a member of Canada's National Task Force on Packaging back in the 1990s, I remember being impressed with what I thought was Europe's apparently far superior *recycling* performance, until I realized that those European *recovery* numbers were padded by materials *recovered* through EFW. When you backed this out, Canadian recyclers were performing just as well as their European counterparts. Still are! That was not the impression that some Canadian government and environmental groups had at the time.[3]

The confusion between *recycling* and *recovery* (and their rates) is unfortunately quite common today. In North America, the terms are often used interchangeably, adding to the confusion. We even call processing centres materials *recovery* facilities not materials *recycling* facilities (which is what they do)![4] The Blue Box programs in the provinces of British Columbia, Saskatchewan, and Manitoba all use the phrase *recovery rate* to describe a material's *recycling* performance. Stewardship Ontario uses both *recycling* rate and *recovery rate* in its reporting documents![5]

None of these programs is focussed on EFW, yet all of them use the word *recovery* for what are specifically *recycling* programs.[6] Confused? If we want to harmonize the measuring of performance, then using the same definitions and terminology within one country would be a good first step!

The United States is struggling with these definitional issues as well in the debate over the Break Free From Plastic Pollution Act. Among other things, this draft legislation specifically excludes chemical recycling (where plastics are broken down to their molecular level to make oils, waxes, new polymers, and other products) from the definition of recycling. Should it be called recycling or recovery? The debate (and the confusion) continues.[7]

Comparisons

Another caution in comparing the performance of recycling programs is ensuring that they account for what they collect in the same way. Ontario, for example, allows mixed broken glass used as a substitute in roadbed aggregate to count as recycling. Australia and the United Kingdom do not.[8]

In the United States, a 2018 study by the Northeast Recycling Council (NERC) noted that 54% of reported glass tonnage from 11 states was sent from materials recovery facilities (MRFs, pronounced "murfs") to glass processors to be cleaned. Some 24% of it ended up as daily cover at landfills, 15% as trash, with 7% used as aggregate, road base, or fill.[9] What, then, counts as recycling? Does recycling only mean bottle-to-bottle? And how do you compare provinces and states that have beverage deposit regimes or bottle bills with ones that don't? Direct comparisons between programs are sometimes not possible.

How do you measure it?

And how exactly is a *recycling rate* determined? Here in North America, we are all over the map. Where do you measure it from? How do you find out what was generated in the first place? From industry surveys? From brand owner and retailer reports to stewardship bodies on what they put into the marketplace? From waste composition studies that are then extrapolated statistically to cover the whole state or province?[10]

And where do you measure the recycling part of the equation? Do you measure it from what is collected at curbside and through depots, as

British Columbia does? Or from where the collected material is dumped on the MRF floor, as Quebec does? Or maybe you measure it from what the MRF compacts into bales and sends on to the end-market after it has been cleaned up a bit in processing, like Ontario?

These are very important distinctions because the more that materials are cleaned up after collection (that is, the more contamination that is removed from them), the lower the recycling rate. The level of contamination, and the quality of the MRF equipment in capturing materials, can make a big difference to the end result.

North American paper recycling mills, for example, now expect paper with very low (less than 5%) non-fibre contamination rates, and some end-markets are demanding even lower than that (less than 2%). The end-markets for plastic, glass, and metal are also pushing back, downgrading materials when higher market specifications are not met.

In the United States, the Environmental Protection Agency has begun a comprehensive data collection assessment with a view to developing a national recycling strategy. Achieving consensus on common definitions and measuring points would be a great start.

Real recycling rates

Of course, what we are talking about here is not really *recycling* rates at all! More like *sent for recycling* rates. This is a crucial clarification because when a material finally arrives at a paper, steel, glass, or plastic recycling plant, not all of it can be used to make a new product. There are always yield, residue, and contamination losses in the remanufacturing process (outlined in more detail in the **RECYCLED** entry).

For this reason, some government policy makers (particularly in Europe) are starting to define recycling as occurring only when materials make it through to the "final recycling process," by which they mean the remanufacturing of the recycled material back into a new product. In effect, they want to remove any "rejects" or contamination and yield losses at the end-market level from the amount that can be claimed to have been recycled.

While this would undoubtedly lead to a truer overall picture of recycling, establishing such a net recycling rate in practice may be more difficult than policymakers think. End-markets typically receive materials from multiple sources, and tracing them accurately could be a problem.

In the meantime, there's a huge need for international and national harmonization of definitions. At the moment, confusion (and a few little green lies) reign supreme. For example, Ontario's much vaunted Blue Box program is reported to have a 57% *recovery* rate (which, as we know now, is really a *sent for recycling* rate based on what is sent from the MRFs to end-markets).

But if you were to take into account the contamination in the bales that the end-markets receive and have to landfill or burn, plus the specific material characteristics that reduce process yields in remanufacturing used materials, then the *real* recycling rate of Ontario's Blue Box *could be 25% lower* than what it's publicly reported to be (57%).[11]

75% - 80%
Ministry's "Diversion Rate"

57%
Reported "Recovery Rate"

32%
Real Recycling Rate?

This presents a political conundrum. Do you pursue and report on *real* Blue Box recycling rates (say, 32%) with all the bad (and ignorant) press that comes with that knowledge? (Governments generally do not like the political optics of lower recycling rates, especially when they have announced with great fanfare that they will achieve much higher recycling rates than the previous administration or a neighbouring jurisdiction). Or do you continue to promote higher and higher recycling targets because "people love their Blue Boxes" and you want them to feel better about "doing something for the environment?"[12]

This is where *what* you measure, and *how* you measure it, feeds into the choices that governments make, and what they tell the public.

As I said at the top, the current ambiguity and confusion over recovery and recycling rates opens the door to the telling of many little (and not so little) green lies.

See also "**RECOVERABLE,**" and **RECYCLED.**

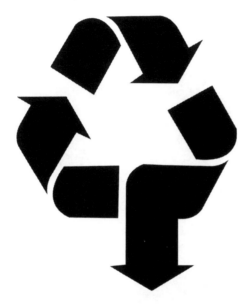

Chapter 24

Recyclable
Lots of little green lies and mass confusion

Let me try to unravel the confusing world of what *recyclable* means. The first thing to understand is that environmental labelling crosses borders. Products and packaging flow freely around the world so marketers face different labelling rules in different countries and have to constantly monitor changes to those rules, which can be an expensive proposition. There are also considerable costs in communicating the varying environmental claims to hundreds of specific marketplaces where products or packaging end up.

To reduce that confusion and cost, most countries base their environmental labelling guidelines on International Organization for Standardization (ISO) documents that countries have hammered out together (ISO 14021: https://www.iso.org/standard/66652.html). The United States and Canada both follow these ISO guidelines when it comes to environmental labelling while offering specific "best practice" advice to Americans and Canadians about what is considered acceptable in their particular marketplaces. The United States has its Federal Trade Commission (FTC) *Green Guides,* and

Canada has its Competition Bureau *Environmental Claims: A Guide for Industry and Advertisers*.[1]

Countries generally follow the ISO guidelines, but when it comes to the crunch (or legal action), individual country rules apply. The product or package you have in your hand may have come from Canada or the United States (or anywhere else), but wherever it ends up is where the guidelines or that country's laws apply.

Another thing: Determining recyclability is but one step on the journey towards actually recycling something. It's really just the first step of five, as illustrated in the table below.

First, you need to clarify what the recyclable claim applies to (whether to a product, packaging, or service) and whether recycling systems and facilities are available to handle it. Since a municipality or service provider won't likely agree to collect a material unless there is a ready market for it, the state of end-markets enters the discussion here too. This is where

The Remanufacturing Process:
From Recyclable to New Product

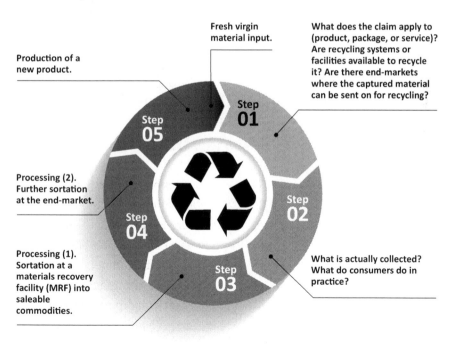

recyclable is determined, where consumers are told what they can do.

The second step in the remanufacturing journey is what consumers actually do in practice because unfortunately we don't always do what we say we're going to do in surveys. Or it's inconvenient for us in some way. Or the promotional and educational material just didn't get to us.

The third and fourth steps in this journey towards a new product involve processing (or removing contamination so that a material can be re-used or recycled). Most residentially collected materials are trucked to a materials recovery facility (MRF, "murf") where materials are divided into different streams depending on their end-market destination, and are sorted and baled for delivery.

There is always a level of contamination that needs to be removed. There are also yield losses and residue at the end-market location that have to be landfilled or sent to alternative fuel or to energy-from-waste facilities by the end-market processors as they finally turn what you sent them into a new product (see **RECYCLED** and **RECOVERY AND RECYCLING RATES**).

That's the big picture. But let's return to the *recyclable* part (**Step 1 highlighted in the table**). The first step in reviewing a claim for recyclability is to determine what exactly the claim applies to. It could apply to the individual product (a camera) or to the packaging it came in (a carton), or both. But any claim "shall be presented in a manner that clearly indicates whether the claim applies to the complete product, or only to a product component or packaging, or to an element of a service." To not do so is false and misleading and deceptive.[2]

The next step is to establish whether systems or facilities exist to actually recycle the product or packaging. Nothing is recyclable if you can't send it on for recycling. The guidelines for both countries are very clear on this. Claims for recyclability "always depend on the existence of (recycling) systems and facilities," says the Canadian guide.[3] The American guidelines are equally clear: "A product or package should not be marketed as recyclable unless it can be collected, separated, or otherwise recovered from the waste stream through an established recycling program for reuse or use in manufacturing or assembling another item."[4]

And both governments have laid out similar parameters for those systems and facilities. The Canadian guidelines say that they must be "conveniently available" to a "reasonable proportion" of purchasers, potential purchasers, and users in the area that the product is to be sold.[5] The US *Green Guides* talk about a "substantial majority" of consumers or communities where the item is sold.[6] (The governments differ slightly in what constitutes a *reasonable proportion* and a *substantial majority*. The *Green Guides* suggest 60%; the Canadian guidelines 50%).

Both governments also divide recyclable claims into what they call "unqualified" claims (by which they mean the product or package meets the 60% or 50% levels noted above) and "qualified" claims (where they don't meet those thresholds). If the levels are not met, then the marketer must indicate this.

The general claim that something is recyclable "where facilities exist" is discouraged in Canada because it's not specific enough.[7] Similarly in the United States, a claim of "Recyclable: check to see if recycling facilities exist in your area" is considered to be too vague and deceptive.[8] The lower the availability to recycling, the more detailed the clarification required.[9]

On these issues, the availability of recycling systems and facilities and qualified and unqualified claims, the two governments are pretty much aligned. It would appear to be relatively straightforward then to establish where these systems and facilities exist in each country, the materials they accept, and whether particular materials meet the 60% and 50% thresholds. And whether claims for "100% Recyclable" can even exist, given that both countries have remote areas where consumers definitely do not have, and likely never will have, "conveniently available" access to recycling (see **HUNDRED (100%) FULLY, COMPLETELY**).

Oh, that things could be that simple! It is really unfortunate that neither the US nor the Canadian guidelines spell out in more plain language that something that is *technically* capable of being recycled doesn't necessarily make it recyclable. This is a major area of confusion, certainly in industry workshops I have run. And if industry people are confused, you can bet that consumers are too![10]

It's great that companies can make products or packaging from recycled materials. They can substantiate and promote that fact. It's a *recycled content* claim.

A *recyclable* claim, however, is fundamentally different. It requires two things: that the product or package (or parts of them) be *technically* capable of being recycled, and that recycling *systems or facilities actually exist* in the area where the product or package ends up. You must have both. You can't claim something is recyclable just because it is technically possible. As the Canadian guideline states: claims for recyclability "*always* (emphasis added) depend on the existence of (recycling) systems and facilities."

The danger of over-emphasizing the technical ability to recycle something is that it shifts the focus away from whether systems and facilities exist to recycle it, and towards the various outcomes of the overall journey towards a new product or package. It puts pressure on industry players to declare a customer's product or packaging *recyclable* when they know full well that a portion of it will never actually be recycled.

Because that's the manufacturing reality. All along the journey, from when the consumer places the product or package in the collection system through the various processing steps, there is contamination to be removed and yield and residue losses to be dealt with. The US *Green Guides* hint at this when it states that a product or package can be recyclable even if "minor incidental components" are not. Does this mean stuff like labels, adhesives, starch, clay? The *Guides* don't say. And how much is minor? 10%? 15%? These are grey areas.[11]

I think it's far smarter to stick simply with the key recyclable parameter of access to recycling systems and facilities (that's what consumers want to know) than to get mixed up in how much collected material actually makes it into a new product or package. That's a whole other little green lie (see **RECYCLED**). And please don't get me started on what I think of "100% Recyclable" claims! I deal with that elsewhere! Check out **HUNDRED (100%) FULLY, COMPLETELY.**

See also **RECYCLED, RECYCLED versus RECYCLABLE, HUNDRED (100%) FULLY, COMPLETELY,** and **RECOVERY AND RECYCLING RATES.**

Chapter 25

Recycled
How much actually gets recycled?

All sorts of people claim they are responsible for recycling materials (municipalities, waste haulers) but what they do, in fact, is play their part in *sending materials on for recycling*, which is something quite different. The only people who do the *actual recycling* are the end-markets (the paper recycling mills, the glass plants, the plastic processors, or the steel and aluminium foundries).

And it's quite a journey from the material you placed in your recycling bin to producing a new product. Right from the start, what you put in your bin, box, or cart, has a big impact on how much of that paper, plastic, glass, or metal can be used later. Because recycling is basically all about reducing contamination so that a material can be used again. Paper mills don't like plastic mixed with their paper. And plastic plants don't like paper labels or other paper mixed with plastics. No one (including glass recyclers) wants crushed glass.

This is why different methods of collection have evolved. Some municipalities collect materials in different streams (usually paper fibres like newspapers, printing and writing paper, corrugated boxes and boxboard cartons in one; and containers made of plastic, glass, and metals in another). Other municipalities collect materials all together in what is called *commingled* or *single-stream* to save on collection costs. And several provinces and states have deposit/refund programs (or bottle bills) for beverage containers as well. It can be confusing, but the instructions on "what goes where" are important because the overall aim is to reduce contamination and to enhance any offsetting revenues for the material.

From your home, the paper, plastic, glass, and metal are trucked to what's called a materials recovery facility (MRF, pronounced "murf"), where the recyclables are thrown onto the floor then shovelled by a front-end loader onto a conveyor belt. This takes them up to a sorting conveyor, the first step in their separation into different material streams, preparing them for their eventual end-markets.

Contaminating items are weeded out; stuff that shouldn't have been put in the recycle bin in the first place such as shoes, umbrellas, and sports equipment. After this pre-sort, special equipment is used to separate the various materials (mixed paper, newspapers, and corrugated boxes, glass, steel, aluminum, each of the various plastic resins, and milk cartons and juice boxes).

Even with all this specialized detection, some material still gets rejected, depending on the ability of the MRF equipment to detect it (black plastics, full-sleeved bottles, and small items that don't get picked up by the machinery or human sorters). According to a recent report based on US state and municipal data, sorting and processing losses can range from 6% for ferrous cans through to 44% for rigid plastics.[1]

Typical Loss and Yield Rates (US)

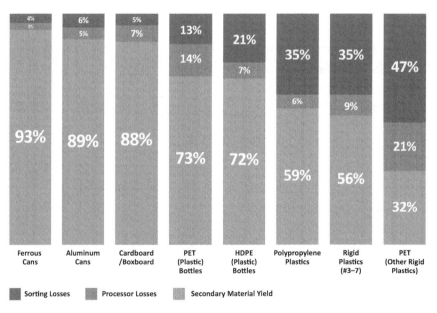

Source: State and municipal data, MRF outputs and bale composition, and Eunomia discussions with material processors (see ENDNOTES, Recycled).

Anecdotal evidence from some Canadian operators indicates processing losses of less than 10%.

But that's not the end of the journey. The processed materials (normally in the form of compacted bales) are finally sent on to the paper recycling mills, the plastic processors, the glass plant, and the steel and aluminium foundries. Here they again go through quality sorts, removing further contamination. In a paper mill, this would be a combination of what are called *out-throws* and *prohibitives*.

Out-throws are paper materials that a particular recycling mill may not want but could be recycled elsewhere. For example, a mill recycling old newspapers doesn't want old corrugated boxes mixed in with its furnish (recipe). *Prohibitives*, on the other hand, are non-paper material (pieces of plastic, glass, and metal). These mill rejects may represent up to 5% of what the mill receives, with most of it having to be burned or landfilled.

Another feature, specific to paper, is what's called *shrink*. When paper fibres get wet in the re-pulping process, they shrink by as much as 10%, so for every 10 tonnes of paper that comes in the door for recycling maybe only 90% is incorporated into a paper product leaving the mill.[2]

Other materials have even higher yield losses, according to the Eunomia study mentioned earlier (see Eunomia chart at left). You can chop maybe 30% off the reported PET bottle recycling rates since PET yields range, at best, between 60% and 70%. Much of the non-PET material is bottle caps, but as these are primarily polypropylene they can be captured and sent on for recycling, reducing the net yield loss for the bale. Still, PET recyclers have to manage 100 tonnes of material to yield only 60 to 70 tonnes of usable product.[3] This is just one reason why recycling plastics is more expensive than using virgin plastics!

And any coloured glass in a flint (clear) glass operation will ruin the whole batch. Normally coloured glass is separated using optical sorters either prior to or at the glass plant. Mixed coloured glass by itself is not necessarily an issue as long as the glass is not so crushed that the optical sorters can't differentiate between the materials.

These few examples indicate why contamination and the supply of clean material to end-markets are such big issues today (especially since several Asian countries have tightened up their waste material import rules). Generally speaking, most plastic, glass, and metal recyclables now go to markets in North America. Paper recyclables are used for domestic consumption but are also widely exported.

So, when municipalities and other levels of government, waste haulers, and MRF operators, puff up their chests to take credit for recycling *x* number of tonnes of material, remember that what you are hearing *is not the full story!* The amount of material that actually makes it into a new product for sale is always less (sometimes much less) than what was delivered to the end-market in the first place.

See also **RECYCLED versus RECYCLABLE** and **RECOVERY AND RECYCLING RATES**.

Chapter 26

Recycled Content
False arguments are being used to promote post-consumer recycled content

Don't get me wrong. I fully support the use of post-consumer material in packaging and products. Just not some of the BS that goes with it. And this is important because companies and governments are stipulating post-consumer recycled content as if it is some sort of gold standard, without knowing all the facts.[1] Here are some of the false claims being made.

Claim 1: That post-consumer recycled is "environmentally better" than pre-consumer recycled content

Setting aside the rather important question of what "environmentally better" actually means, I am not aware of any scientific evidence that one is better than the other. In fact, they are really the same material, just coming from different places along the feedstock supply chain.

Part of the problem is that some people think that pre-consumer is simply industrial scrap. *It is not.* The scrap at a paper mill, for example, is called broke, the paper material that occasionally breaks in a paper machine during the papermaking process and that is thrown back into the pulper (a big washing machine, if you like) for further recycling. *Mill broke is not considered, or claimed, as recycled content.* (In the plastics industry, this material is called regrind. In the glass industry, culls).

From the paper mill, the roll of paper or board is generally shipped to a converting plant that is closer to the end-market for the material. Here the actual paper or board is cut and shaped and perhaps folded and glued before being shipped on to a distributor or maybe even the final consumer.

In the process of cutting and shaping the paper or board at the converting plant, there is always a small percentage of off-cuts, like the trim left over after a sewing pattern is cut from cloth. These off-cuts, which could be envelope clippings, corrugated cuttings, or boxboard trim, are called pre-consumer because they do not go to the end-consumer. It is perfectly good material, though, like the sewing trim, and is sold and shipped back to a mill for recycling. It is not wasted.

Post-consumer paper or board, on the other hand, is the complete paper product ready for sale (a newspaper, magazine, writing pad, corrugated box, boxboard carton, or a paper bag) that ends up in a factory, supermarket, office or home, and is later collected for recycling. It's also sold back to a recycling mill, just like the pre-consumer material.

There is no difference, then, in the way that pre-consumer and post-consumer paper or board is originally manufactured in a mill. It is exactly the same material (like the sewing off-cuts) with the same environmental production inputs. The only difference is that they come back to the mill from a different place in the recovered paper feedstock supply chain.

In their rush to promote the greater use of recycled content paper, however, some environmental groups have encouraged the misleading perception that post-consumer material is somehow environmentally superior. US-based Environmental Defense, for example, claimed some 20 years ago that "buying paper with post-consumer recycled content achieves direct reductions in wood, water and energy use, release of pollutants during manufacturing, and solid waste and greenhouse gas emissions from paper decomposing in landfills."

All of this is true. But it's equally true of pre-consumer content. You could even argue that pre-consumer content is "better" because it doesn't go to landfill. It requires a lot less energy to collect, sort, clean, and transform than post-consumer material, which tends to be more contaminated. Yet some environmental groups, business corporations, and even governments continue to peddle the little green lie that post-consumer content is somehow environmentally superior. It is not.

Claim 2: That post-consumer is "more circular" than pre-consumer

One popular line I have heard is that pre-consumer "is not a fully-fledged member of the circular economy" and that "only post-consumer embodies the circular economy."² This is BS. Isn't the circular economy all about minimizing waste? So, what could be more circular than minimizing waste at the converting stage?

> **Isn't the circular economy all about minimizing waste (wherever it occurs)?**

Pre-consumer material is like the sewing trim mentioned above. It's what's left over after you have cut the pattern from cloth. Since you've already paid for the cloth, you ensure your design makes maximum use of the cloth you have. And what you have left over, you send back (in the paper industry's case) to a mill, to be incorporated into another recycled content product. Nothing is wasted. It doesn't go to landfill. Sounds pretty circular to me. I think this BS arises because most waste management policy (and political attention) is focussed on the waste from households, and not on what happens in normal industrial manufacturing processes.

Claim 3: That post-consumer is "better" because it replaces virgin material

Hogwash! Both pre-consumer and post-consumer replace virgin material. Both were made in a mill (once) and both are now recycled again (potentially many times).

And now for the unintended consequences of pushing 100% post-consumer content. If a company or a government specifies only 100% post-consumer, what's going to happen? Some suppliers may be able to produce only 100% post-consumer, but what about those off-cuts I mentioned earlier coming to the recycling mill from other customers? What's the mill supposed to do with them now? *Dump them?* That would not exactly meet the ideals of a circular economy now, would it?

There are also the physical limitations of the material to bear in mind. Wood fibres, for example, can only be recycled between four and nine times before they become too short and thin to be used again. So, if all paper was required to be 100% recycled content, it wouldn't be too long before you couldn't make paper at all. An infusion of virgin fibre is always required somewhere in the system to keep the whole recycling loop going, to keep fibres strong and able to perform their designed intent.

The same applies to plastics, which typically can be mechanically recycled about seven times before their chemical and physical characteristics change too much and they can't be recycled any more. Virgin plastics will always be required, at least until chemical recycling is mainstream.

So, what's the solution for a company wanting to promote greater use of recycled content? By all means, specify a recycled content number, but give the industry the flexibility to meet the target by not specifying how much should be pre-consumer and how much post-consumer. There is far less pre-consumer material out there (because companies are economically motivated to reduce their production costs, to be efficient, to be circular). And once that pre-consumer trim is gone, it's gone.

If companies need more recycled content to make their products or packaging, they'll be forced to get it from post-consumer sources. That's how the market works. That's why the corrugated box industry, for example, started targeting residential sources of used paper decades ago. It couldn't get enough paper to recycle from industrial sources.

See also **HUNDRED (100%) FULLY, COMPLETELY.**

Chapter 27

Recycled *versus* Recyclable
They are not the same thing!

Recycled can mean either "sent on for recycling" (that is the intention) or "turned into a new product." *Recyclable* is something quite different. It means "being able to physically put something out for recycling."

Here's an example to illustrate the difference. Most of the Blue Box materials currently collected from Ontario homes are widely recyclable, according to the Canadian Competition Bureau guidelines on environmental labelling and advertising. What that means is that at least 50% of Ontario households with Blue Box or depot service, can put those materials out for recycling. (In the United States, the Federal Trade Commission has a 60% access level for use of the recyclable claim).

As you can see by the table (overleaf), six materials are considered recyclable for every household that the Ontario program covers: aluminum food and beverage cans; glass bottles and jars; newspapers; polyethylene terephthalate (PET) plastic food and beverage bottles; steel food and beverage cans; and corrugated boxes). Several other materials have high access rates too: boxboard cartons; high density polyethylene (HDPE) containers; other plastic containers; aluminum foil; gable top and aseptic cartons; and steel paint cans -- all the way down to polystyrene foam at 63% access.[1]

What that means is that Ontario householders have been told that they can put these materials out to the curb for recycling. They have *access* to recycling: therefore, those particular materials are recyclable, according to the federal guidelines.

But that does not mean that householders actually do put them out for recycling (the road to recycling is paved with good intentions); or that they were sent on for recycling; or that they were ever recycled into a new product.

"Recyclable" does not mean recycled

Material	"Recyclable" % households with access to program	Sent on for Recycling % material actually collected and sent on for recycling
Aluminum food and beverage cans	100%	46.8%
Glass bottles and jars	100%	68.0%
Newsprint	100%	79.6%
PET bottles, food, beverage	100%	55.2%
Steel food and beverage cans	100%	69.8%
Corrugated boxes	100%	98.0%
Boxboard cartons	99.9%	61.9%
HDPE containers	99.8%	53.7%
Other plastic containers	99.5%	33.9%
Aluminum foil	99.3%	3.2%
Gable top cartons	98.4%	55.6%
Aseptic cartons	96.7%	29.5%
Steel paint cans	94.4%	7.1%
Steel aerosols	88.2%	31.4%
Polystyrene crystal	82.8%	4.3%
HDPE/LDPE film	71.0%	9.7%
Polystyrene foam	63.4%	4.3%

Sources: Resource Productivity & Recovery Authority (RPRA) Datacall Report 2018; Stewardship Ontario, Blue Box Generation and Recovery Table 2018.

For example, more than 99% of Ontario households with Blue Box service in 2018 could place aluminum foil in their Blue Boxes, which is great. But only 3% of foil was actually collected and sent on for recycling. Similarly with steel paint cans. More than 94% of households were *able to* recycle them, but only 7% were *sent on* for recycling. And polystyrene foam. Over 60% of Ontario households had access to its recycling (which is quite impressive), but only 4% was sent on for recycling.

Unfortunately, there are opportunities here for greenwashing, for standing back and saying that a material is recyclable and that it meets all the guidelines to be able to claim the coveted recyclable logo in its marketing and sales pitches, while doing little to encourage residents to actually put more of that material out for recycling and thereby increasing its capture and sent for recycling rate.

So be wary of claims (whether in the United States or Canada) that a material with a high access rate to recycling facilities is actually captured for recycling, or ever makes it into a new product.

See also **RECYCLED, RECYCLABLE,** and **RECOVERY AND RECYCLING RATES**.

Chapter 28

Recycling
To those who say "Recycling is dead," I say BS

Every Tuesday night I come face-to-face with the twin issues of consumption and sustainable materials management or the latest buzzword favoured by governments and some corporations: *circular economy*.[1] For this Tuesday night is Recycling and Composting Night. Why did I buy that stuff? Did I really need it? What about the packaging? What do I do with it now?

From the bathroom and the bedroom, I gather toilet rolls and tissue, envelopes and writing paper. From the kitchen and dining room, I grab the box of recyclables holding old newspapers, cartons, cans, jars and bottles; the separate container for food scraps under the sink; and the small "garbage" bag of other stuff. Then I head for the large carts parked in the garage before wheeling the appropriate ones for this week (recycling and organics) out to the curb for the morning pick-up. All told, it takes me maybe five or ten minutes. And I feel good about doing my little bit for the circular economy.

Feeling good is important. Because successful recycling requires collective participation and the sense that your little contribution is valued and worth the effort. Having worked in the paper industry, I know where this material goes and how important it is to the local paper mills who will turn it into something new.

Where I live, more than 70% of all household paper is sent on for recycling, most of it to packaging mills that produce 100% recycled content boxes and cartons that are then used to ship Ontario goods within the province and around Canada, or to the United States and other places. This is an unheralded and unspectacular circular economy that's existed for decades, and one that gets no credit from most of the loud and ignorant advocates of "Recycling is dead." Paper is by far the major material being sent on for recycling in both the United States and Canada.[2]

Few of these *"Recycling is dead"* bandwagoners consider the alternatives and the avoided costs of not recycling. If that paper was not sent on for recycling, where would the mills get the feedstock that they need to make new boxes? Ah yes, freshly cut trees! More extraction of resources and use of energy. And how much more quickly would residents' favourite spot (the local landfill) have to be upgraded to take the extra material? Or a brand-new landfill sited using valuable farmland as a new hole to dump waste in? Do you know anyone voting for higher municipal taxes? Or wanting more methane and carbon dioxide emissions from extra paper and organics decaying in landfill? Just what we need in these days of rapid climate change![3]

Sure, there are problems. It frustrates me that more perfectly recyclable paper (mostly writing paper and boxboard or paperboard cartons) is not collected from households; that a lot of people don't know that you still need to separate material types as much as possible to give them a decent chance of actually being recycled; that throwing everything together in one container (commingling or single-stream) does have some advantages (it's easy for the householder and lowers collection costs), but that it's transformed us all into lazy participants (throw it all together and let someone else sort it out); that we have lost sight of the fact that recycling is a remanufacturing process; that contamination, yield losses, and residue go hand-in-hand with making almost anything.

The keys to successful recycling are right there: planning, engineering, and encouragement. To be successful, recycling first has to be convenient. The planning folks have to make it simple. Provide a box, a bag, a cart, a deposit-return system, whatever works for the particular material being recycled, but make it relatively simple. And then continuously educate people on how to use it. Remember that a flick of a wrist determines whether something ends up in the recycling or in the trash. Recycling won't happen without consumers wanting to make the effort.[4]

It's the engineering team's job to figure out how to take that mix of materials set out in carts or whatever and to separate the valuable commodities at the materials recovery facility (MRF) before they are sent on to the end-markets to be recycled into new products or packaging.

Of course, one of the key obstacles to greater recycling success in North America is the relative cost to landfill. Where's the economic incentive to recycle, to establish a more circular economy (which is what many governments say they want), when landfilling materials is so much cheaper than recycling them? Who determines landfill policies? In many cases, it's the same governments that are loudly pronouncing how important it is that we "transition to a circular economy" as quickly as possible![5]

The "Recycling is dead" folks do have some grounds for complaint with plastics, especially that mixed bag of resin codes 3 to 7. Apart from deposit-return programs in North America, where plastics, glass, and metal do very well, plastics recycling is lagging way behind everyone else. Way behind.[6]

After 18 years of a Blue Box program that's been partially funded by Ontario industry, six materials remain stubbornly in last place: polystyrene, plastic film, aluminum foil, laminated plastic and paper, and steel paint cans. Each of them has achieved abysmal *sent for recycling* rates (12% or lower) over a long period. Basically, there has been no improvement over 18 years.[7] And with the current hate on for plastics, I can understand why some people (a few media columnists among them) are loudly proclaiming that "Recycling is dead" and that the Great Blue Box experiment has failed. This is a short-sighted and narrow view, in my opinion.

The Blue Box experiment has certainly not failed its largest single component: paper. Paper products represent 61% of what's available in households where I live and over 70% of what's sent on for recycling. They also provide 42% of material revenues.[8]

Yes, recycling costs money, but *not to recycle* costs more. It's a bit like paying your energy bill. You always end up paying for the service, but there are ways to reduce how much you pay (by using a dimmer switch, turning the heat down, the lights off, using a thermostat). You can offset recycling costs by making it more efficient and effective, but there are always costs. Yes, recycling may cost you, but it's not dead!

See also **GENERATION (OF WASTE), PACKAGING WASTE, RECYCLED, and WASTE (DEFINITIONS)**.

Chapter 29

Responsible Sourcing (Chain-Of-Custody Certification)
Only buy from certified sources

It would be remiss of me in a consumers' guide on greenwash, lies, fudges, and BS not to give credit where credit is due, to the anti-greenwash forces as it were. One of these is the development of responsible sourcing programs where claims are audited and verified in exchange for an appropriate logo and attendant publicity.

Of course, some of these logo programs are open to abuse,[1] but one model that seems to be reasonably well respected is chain-of-custody certification for forest products. Born out of concerns about illegal logging in tropical countries, chain-of-custody certification is now recognized by a global alliance of retailers and brand owners as one of several key metrics by which their material suppliers will be judged and selected.[2]

Chain-of-custody certification offers proof that wood, paper, and paper packaging is made from raw materials in certified forests, from certified sources, or from certified recycled content. This documented paper trail is audited and verified by independent third parties.

In North America, four organizations offer forest and paper chain-of-custody certification: the Programme for the Endorsement of Forest Certification (PEFC), the Canadian Standards Association (CSA), the Forest Stewardship Council (FSC), and the Sustainable Forestry Initiative (SFI).

Chapter 30

Reusable

Reusable is good but it's not always "better" than recycling

We all know the 3Rs mantra: *reduction* first, followed by *reuse*, and then *recycling*. The problem with mantras, though, is that we can become too rigid in applying them. They should really be seen as a general guidance tool rather than as an absolute *must-do-first*.

Reuse systems do have some clear advantages. Think of glass bottles being washed and reused again and again in deposit-return systems for beverage containers. Or reusable shopping bags that you bring to the store every time you go for groceries. In both cases, you are avoiding the immediate environmental impact of manufacturing a new glass bottle or a shopping bag.

But assessing the overall environmental burden of something is not quite as simple as that. Reuse systems may reduce the need to extract raw materials to make a new container as often as before, but they also add fresh impacts when materials have to be constantly gathered together and cleaned and washed in readiness for reuse. There are environmental burdens in doing this: the use of fuels and transport to pick them up, and then washing and sanitizing them with water and chemicals so they are safe to use again. The number of times the containers are reused (how many trips they take) also becomes a key factor in life-cycle comparisons.

The plastic bag industry has long complained that reusable bags are a health hazard because consumers generally don't wash them on a regular basis or store them unclean in the trunks of their cars, and that at the end of their life most reusable bags are not recyclable.[1] And years ago, the same industry complained that while reuse *seemed* environmentally friendlier,

the single-use, one-way pack was often the better alternative.

More recently, the plastics industry (or at least the sector of it promoting reusable crates) has lobbied the opposite way: that reuse systems are far better for the environment than one-way recyclable packaging. Here's an example I am familiar with that outlines the complexities of the environmental trade-offs involved in the reuse/recycling debate.

Fresh fruit and vegetables in North America are primarily delivered from farm to retailer in a corrugated shipping box. The box is always new (for health and safety reasons) but that doesn't mean it's made from virgin material. It could have anywhere from 0 to 100% recycled content. And once the retailer has finished with it, the box is baled with others and shipped off to a recycling mill to be made into a new box, in a continuous recycling loop. The retailer receives payment for the used boxes.

The competing reusable plastic crate (RPC) system, on the other hand, is based on using the same crate over and over, washing and sanitizing it between uses, and then shipping it off for use by another customer.

Both the paper and the plastic industries have commissioned life-cycle analyses (LCAs) to examine the pros and cons of this issue. The most recent of these, commissioned by the Corrugated Packaging Council, seems the most credible to date. The LCA was peer-reviewed and meets all the other

ISO requirements for such analyses. And its conclusion? Neither system had the overall advantage in all environmental impact categories.

The box was ahead on some, the crate on others. The study recommended that growers and packers not adopt a "one-system fits all" perspective. Much depended on what particular fruit or vegetable was being shipped, where it was being shipped (freight distance), and other variables in the supply chain. Basically, it was a draw from an environmental point of view.[2]

Reuse systems do face increasing concerns, however, over the effectiveness of their sanitization efforts. A recent technical study, published in the international peer reviewed journal *Food Control*, showed how salmonella can become established on reusable produce crates and survive the typical sanitation cycles applied to decontaminate the crates between uses. The surviving salmonella transferred to and from fresh produce on the crate, underscoring the potential for crates to spread the pathogen throughout the supply chain.[3]

The moral of this story? Don't get stuck on mantras. And one system does not fit all.

Chapter 31

Sugarcane (Bagasse)
Be wary of the sweet talk, bagasse is not waste

Sugarcane has been grown in tropical and subtropical countries and warmer climates for thousands of years as a source of a natural sweetener: sugar. Large-scale plantations became more common in the 18th century, with the first American use of bagasse (the fibrous residue left after the sugar juices are extracted) to make paper in 1884.

The first pulp and paper mill using bagasse was built in Braithwaite, Louisiana, in 1898, but the initial experiment was a complete failure. By the 1950s, however, new technologies had emerged to produce good-quality paper from bagasse, and bagasse papermaking is now well established in many countries. More recently, sugar and bagasse have been used to produce ethanol, bioplastics, and moulded pulp products such as food packaging.[1]

There are several claims made for sugarcane bagasse that require closer examination.

Claim 1: Sugarcane bagasse is acid-free

This is true, but it's not exclusive to sugarcane or bagasse-based paper. Acid-free is standard today for *all paper*, including paper made from trees.

There was a time in the late 19th century when wood paper wasn't acid-free because of the natural acids in wood pulp. Librarians around the world became increasingly concerned over the years as the yellowing pages disintegrated in the archives. The initial solution was to add chemicals to counteract the natural acids in the pulp, and later to use precipitated calcium carbonate as a filler material. The less acid in the paper, the longer it can be preserved.

Today, there are two standards for acid-free paper: the American National Standards Institute (ANSI) Z39-48-1992 which establishes "criteria for coated and uncoated paper to last several hundred years," and an equivalent international standard (ISO 9706). Companies meeting these standards can display a circled infinity symbol. There is also an international standard for archival paper.[2]

Claim 2: Historically, bagasse was burned in the cane fields, creating air pollution

This is not true. What has historically been burned in the fields prior to the sugar cane harvest is not bagasse but rather what's called field trash (the tops and leaves of the sugarcane that don't contain any sugar juices).

Traditionally, the fields were first burned pre-harvest to chase out poisonous snakes, rodents, and insects that could attack the cane cutters. But there were strong economic reasons for doing so as well. Burning the field trash not only reduced how much material needed to be transported to the sugar mill, it also created local jobs. Colombian sugarcane fields, for example, are all manually harvested like this because it employs many people.

Where harvesting is mechanized, the purpose is the same: to reduce the cost of transporting biomass to the sugar mill and to reduce the tillage requirements on the cane fields. Some harvesters burn the field trash prior to harvest, some after. One operator in Argentina doesn't do any burning of field trash, just bales it up after harvest and uses it as fuel in its boilers.[3]

In Florida and Louisiana, where harvesting is mechanized, there is extensive pre-harvest burning of the cane standing in the fields to remove the field trash. The local Sierra Club is trying to stop this because it creates air pollution, respiratory problems, and water quality issues with ash and field runoff.[4] It is the burning of the field trash that creates the pollution, not the bagasse. The bagasse is the fibrous residue that's left *after* the cane has been crushed and the sugar juices removed at the sugar mill.

Claim 3: Sugarcane bagasse is waste

No, it is not. The field trash is the waste. Traditionally, bagasse has been used as a fuel in the sugar mill's boilers to make steam and power to run the sugar mill. Sometimes a mill will burn more bagasse than is needed, which saves on landfilling costs. Other times, the excess bagasse is used to generate electricity, which can then be sold to the local power grid for a profit.

In the 1940s and 1950s, more and more sugar mills began to consider shipping the bagasse they were using as energy to those nearby pulp and paper mills that were willing to use bagasse pulp to make paper. And that's where it gets interesting. Because if a sugar mill sends its bagasse on to a paper mill, it now needs something else, an alternative energy fuel, to power the sugar mill.

What the sugar mills end up doing depends on alternative fuel cost and availability. In Colombia, it would be relatively good-quality thermal coal. In Egypt, Iran and Pakistan it's Bunker C fuel oil. In India and China, the choice is usually low-quality thermal brown coal with a higher sulphur content, so emissions would include sulphur dioxide that causes acid rain. Which leads us directly to the fourth claim commonly made by the promoters of bagasse.

Claim 4: That bagasse is "environmentally friendlier" than harvesting trees

Every single life-cycle analysis (LCA) that I have seen comparing bagasse with a paper product considers bagasse to be a "waste" material that is landfilled or burned. *This is not true.* It is not wasted. It is burned for a very good reason (to power the sugar mill). And when it's not burned, and shipped on to a paper mill to make bagasse paper instead, none of these LCAs include the carbon dioxide emissions that result from burning the fossil fuel that's now used to power the sugar mill, the replacement for the carbon-neutral bagasse that was used before.

Sugar Sheet, for example, claims that every two boxes of its copy paper "saves one tree." But the LCA study that this claim is based on falsely considers bagasse as an agricultural waste that would otherwise be disposed of, and fails to account for coal substitution as well.[5]

There is also the question of comparative LCA scope. If a paper product's life cycle

> "Impacts from raw material use were assumed to be reduced for Sugar Sheet paper since the key raw material (bagasse) is an agricultural waste product which would otherwise be disposed."
>
> LCA claim for Sugar Sheet

extends to the environmental impact of the original growing of a tree (even if only sawmill residues are used to make the actual paper product), doesn't that mean that a bagasse-paper product's life cycle *equally extends* to how the sugarcane was grown, and the burning of field trash prior to cane transport to the sugar mill? This field burning would have a major impact on the relative "friendliness" or otherwise of the bagasse product. A cradle-to-grave LCA includes *every* single unit process in the life cycle of the finished product.

There is also some question as to whether all aspects of the shipping of bagasse pulp to North America are being taken into account. For example, virgin bagasse pulp may originally be produced in the Middle East or Asia, but then it's shipped to China for thermoforming before the moulded product is later shipped on to North America.

Are the emissions from the journey prior to arriving in China taken into account in the LCA? And what is the original mill process? How exactly is the original mill making its bagasse market pulp? Are dioxins being discharged in its effluent? What type of bleaching was used? What exactly is in the bagasse pulp being imported from China?

In the meantime, we get claims from bagasse promoters that bagasse is "better" than the alternatives. Eco Kloud, for example, sells a line of bagasse products: bowls, clamshells, cups, plates, and trays. The same lines appear on each entry on its website: "Bagasse sugarcane (bowls and plates etc.) are much better alternative to Styrofoam (non-degradable), plastic (non-biodegradable, petroleum based, pollutant) and paper (cutting trees)." [6]

No explanatory statements are offered to the consumer; there are no descriptions of the methods used to make the comparisons; there are no results presented from any published standards or recognized test method; and no details given of the assumptions made in the comparative assertions.

Failure to offer this information to consumers would seem to be a clear breach of the guidelines set out by the Competition Bureau (Canada)[7] and the US Federal Trade Commission.[8]

See also **"TREE-FREE."**

Chapter 31

Sustainable
By itself, this word means nothing.
Look for credible management systems

Sustainability is a very complex goal because it encompasses a broad range of environmental, social, and economic factors that can only be measured over a long period of time.

The *environmental* part of it alone often involves resource use and consumption in which a peer-reviewed life-cycle analysis that meets ISO 14040 standards would be the bare minimum just to get started. So, generally speaking, be very wary about broad claims that something is sustainable.[1]

There are, however, some credible management systems that focus on a *specific aspect* of sustainability. For example, sustainable forest management. And in this, North America leads the world.

Sustainable forest management (SFM) looks at the forest for *all* of its values: social, economic, environmental, and cultural. It considers not just the wood harvested and local employment, but also the streams protected and the wildlife habitat conserved.[2] And it provides assurances that forest products are sourced from sustainably managed forests. It's also backed up by government laws, regulations, and policies.[3]

The idea of sustainable forest management came to the fore at the 1992 United Nations Conference on the Environment and Development in Rio de Janeiro, Brazil (the "Earth Summit"). Following the conference, 12 countries including Canada, the United States, and Mexico, formed what became known internationally as the Montreal Process.

By 1995, these countries had agreed to use "a common set of science-based indicators that would give government, industry, researchers and the public a way to consistently define, assess, monitor and report progress on the sustainable management" of their forests. Collectively, the countries represent 90% of the world's temperate and boreal forests, 49% of all forests, 58% of planted forests, 49% of global roundwood production, and 31% of the world's population.[4] That's a pretty impressive group of countries and a solid achievement.

Today, almost half of Canada's total forest land is certified by independent third parties as being sustainably managed.[5] Canada, in fact, leads the world in the amount of forest independently certified as sustainably managed and is currently home to some 35% of the world's certified forest, way ahead of all other countries. The United States is currently in third place behind Russia.[6]

In North America, the major recognized certifying bodies are the Sustainable Forestry Initiative (SFI), the Forest Stewardship Council (FSC), the Canadian Standards Association (CSA), the Programme for the Endorsement of Forest Certification (PEFC), and the American Tree Farm System (ATFS).

See also **RESPONSIBLE SOURCING (CHAIN-OF-CUSTODY CERTIFICATION)**.

Chapter 32
Toilet Paper
Smear campaign on tissue paper gives consumers a bum steer

Some environmental campaigns (not all) typically demonize their target using exaggeration, hyperbole, and just plain false information. Like Trump with Mexicans, Muslims, and fine white supremacists. And the more gullible media usually play sucker and tag along.

This is certainly true of a recent campaign against tissue paper and towelling launched by the New York based Natural Resources Defense Council (NRDC) and STAND.earth (formerly ForestEthics). Their target is Canadian production of tissue paper, and their aim is to persuade companies such as Procter & Gamble, Kimberly-Clark, and Georgia-Pacific to move from virgin to recycled fibre or to alternatives like wheat straw and bamboo.[1]

I have no problem with questioning the use of tissue paper in the first place, although NRDC's revelation that people once used corn cobs to clean themselves up some 150 years ago fills me with some amazement. A bidet never looked so attractive!

Nor do I have a problem with discussing the relative environmental merits and performance of various types of fibre (virgin, recycled, wheat straw, and bamboo), although I would insist that any comparative life-cycle analysis meet ISO 14040 standards (including a publicly available, independent third-party review).[2]

I do have a problem, however, with how these two groups characterize and demonize not only the tissue sector but also, by implication, the whole Canadian forest and paper industries. Readers are left with a falsely grim doomsday picture of Canadian tissue production.

The campaign talks about "flushing forests down the toilet'" and logging "seven National Hockey league rinks each minute." Sounds terrible, but how about some facts? Facts like:

- 99.8% of Canada's forest lands are *not* logged in an average year.[3]
- 99.8% of Canada's boreal forest is *not* logged in an average year.[4]
- The main object of logging operations is for lumber (to build houses, schools, and hospitals), not tissue paper. The Forest Products Association of Canada estimates that less than 1% of total harvested wood (not just from the boreal) ends up in toilet paper.[5]
- By provincial law, any harvested area must be successfully regenerated after harvest.
- Much of Canada's forest lands are independently certified as being sustainably managed, including by a certifier (the Forest Stewardship Council, or FSC) whose credentials these very same environmental groups regularly promote.[6]

NRDC and STAND.earth also claim in their tissue report that "clearcutting decimates the ecosystem."[7] Why are they supporting and promoting the Forest Stewardship Council then? FSC certification standards allow for clear-cutting by forest management companies (see **HYPOCRISY?**).

They also advance the false argument that post-consumer paper is "environmentally better" than pre-consumer paper,[8] and give the impression that most tissue paper in Canada is made from "centuries-old trees" hewn from the Canadian boreal. Sorry, folks. Only 1%, yes, only 1% of trees in the Canadian boreal is more than 200 years old.[9] Facts do matter. Get the real poop next time!

See also **"ANCIENT" FORESTS, BOREAL FOREST, HYPOCRISY?, RECYCLED CONTENT, and "TREE-FREE."**

Chapter 33

"Tree-Free"

Fast and loose with the facts, and a questionable wheat straw model

A Canadian environmental group has launched a smear campaign against paper packaging while promoting its replacement by wheat straw. What are the facts?

First, some background. Paper was made from *non-wood* materials like papyrus, parchment, hemp, flax, rattan, mulberry, bamboo, rice straw, and even seaweed long before it was made from wood,[1] so it would be hypocritical of me or the paper industry to criticize the investigation and use of what are generally marketed today as "tree-free" alternatives.

In fact, it was less than 200 years ago that a young Nova Scotian named Charles Fenerty pulped some local spruce and sent it on to a publisher for evaluation as a possible replacement for the old linen and rags that were then used to make paper. It would take another 25 years before the first groundwood pulp would be produced in Canada, and a little longer before wood became the papermaking material of choice in North America.[2]

Interest in alternatives to wood has continued over the years, however, with various trials taking place to establish land preparation and harvesting procedures; to assess plant yields and the suitability of crop residues for papermaking; and to sort out the quantities and locations of the fibre needed. Bamboo, kenaf, hemp, and straw emerged as the most likely candidates.

And there have been some successes. In the 1940s, 25 mills in the US Midwest produced almost 1 million tons of corrugating medium (used in the making of corrugated boxes) from straw. "Momentum in the non-wood fiber industry was lost, however, following the [Second World War] because of the high costs of gathering and processing straw, and the return to pulping of hardwoods [by] the paper industry. The last straw mill in the U.S. closed in 1960."[3]

The advocates and promoters persisted, however. In June 2010, investors in Prairie Pulp and Paper announced their intention to build a commercial-scale wheat and flax straw mill in rural Manitoba, Canada. They persuaded Staples to stock their copy paper, an 80%/20% wheat straw/wood-fibre blend that they were then importing from India.[4] Public relations people and influencers enthused over the concept, journalists wrote gushing copy,[5] and a celebrity promoter (actor Woody Harrelson) made simplistic and inaccurate claims for Prairie Pulp. The venture fell apart.

More recently, in September 2017, Columbia Pulp finalized its funding and held a ground-breaking ceremony for its new wheat and alfalfa-straw mill in Starbuck, Washington. The Canadian-based environmental group Canopy, which has wholeheartedly supported both recent ventures, was delighted at Columbia Pulp's proposed move to make packaging and moulded pulp from agricultural residues.[6]

Canopy smears paper, promotes alternatives

The paper industry has no problem with the use of alternative fibres and, in fact, uses wheat straw and other alternatives frequently as additives in the wood paper-making process. The paper industry does, however, get a little upset when the marketers and promoters of non-wood fibre such as wheat straw ignore, disparage, and/or badmouth the existing paper industry infrastructure to advance their cause. Vancouver-based Canopy, in particular, has clearly adopted a strategy of smearing wood-based packaging while heavily promoting Columbia Pulp's wheat straw venture and others like it.

It was no coincidence that prior to announcing their grand vision of replacing the world's wood-pulp mills with some 200 mills using agricultural residues and fibre crops instead,[7] that Canopy would launch a global campaign against paper packaging (the very same market Columbia Pulp was targeting for its wheat straw).

Canopy's campaign launch was full of emotional rhetoric. Every year, it claimed, 3 billion trees "disappear into packaging," leaving "a trail of deforestation, degraded forest systems, threatened species, and an increasingly volatile climate."[8] Canopy has continued this emotional smear attack despite paper industry protestations that many of its claims (especially as they relate to Canada and the United States) are just plain wrong or blatantly misleading.[9] Here are some of them.

Claim 1: The "3 billion' trees"
Canopy's claim that "3 billion" trees are harvested every year for packaging, of course, is intended as a dramatic global symbol rather than an accurate accounting of how many trees are actually used for packaging. I mean, does one large tree equal 20 spindly ones? It is not easy doing these calculations, and Canopy doesn't enlighten us with how it got to 3 billion. The impression it wants to leave, of course, is that 3 billion is a *huge* number. And a *terrible* waste. So please send a donation.

What are the facts? According to the US Forest Service, there are some 365 billion trees in US forests. Slightly more than Canopy's 3 billion![10] The North American boreal zone by itself holds some 500 billion individual trees, according to a scientific article in *Frontiers and Forests and Global Change*.[11] And the International Boreal Conservation Campaign has just released a video claiming there are 600 billion trees in the Canadian boreal alone. This is not even counting the rest of the world's forests!

Canopy goes further. It implies that its "3 billion" trees go into packaging and that's it. Nothing else happens.

Claim 2: That 3 billion trees "disappear into packaging"
Canopy generally fails to mention the fact that new trees are planted to regenerate any forest that's been harvested for packaging. This is certainly the case in Canada, where governments own more than 90% of the forest lands. Logged areas must be successfully regenerated after harvest, either naturally or artificially (through tree planting and seeding).

Canadian foresters on average replant just less than 1,000 new seedlings a minute.[12] Canopy fails to mention this when it badmouths paper packaging (even though it promotes sustainable forest management, which includes replanting trees, through its support of the Forest Stewardship Council).

Instead, it largely focuses on telling the public and its supporters only how many trees are allegedly cut down, and mentions nothing about the legal requirements (and the business sense) in regenerating harvested areas so that the forest resource is there for the future. No, these trees just "disappear into packaging."

Then there's this:

Claim 3: That most paper boxes are made from virgin market pulp.[13] In fact, very little virgin pulp is used by Canadian mills to make boxes in Canada. That's because most boxes are 100% recycled content.[14] They are not made (as Canopy implies) with the "habitat of endangered species such as orangutans or caribou." They are made from old used boxes collected from the back of Canadian factories and supermarkets, from offices, and from Canadian homes. And that's been the case for 30, 40, 50 years or so. So no, paper packaging does not have "a crushing footprint" on the world's forests, biodiversity and climate.

In fact, the Canadian industry led North America, and perhaps the world, in pioneering the further recycling of used cereal and shoe boxes back in the 1990s. I know this because I headed the environmental council that coordinated it. Today, some 94% of Canadians can recycle a material that used to go straight to landfill.[15]

Most Canadian packaging board now 100% recycled content

Most of the paper packaging made by Canadian mills today is 100% recycled content. Old corrugated boxes and cartons are collected from the back of factories and supermarkets; used paper from offices; and a wide range of paper material gathered and sorted from residential (Blue Box) programs across the country.

Source: The Paper & Paperboard Packaging Environmental Council press release, 2019

"Did you know that three billion trees are cut down every year for paper packaging? That means thousand-year-old forests are being destroyed to make boxes."

Source: Canopy's Pack4Good Campaign, 2020.

"TREE-FREE" | 135

Claim 4: That packaging leaves "a trail of deforestation"
This is a gross distortion of fact. Canada has one of the lowest rates of deforestation in the world *(less than 1%)*. Nor is forestry the major cause of deforestation in Canada. That "honour" goes to the conversion of forest land to agriculture (see **DEFORESTATION**).

In fact, the specific deforestation rate for forestry as a whole in Canada is a mere 0.0004% (yes, that's three zeroes and a four).[16] A*nd guess what, paper packaging is not responsible for any of it!* That's because unlike Canopy's BS about "1000-year-old trees" being used to make shipping, pizza and shoe boxes,[17] most of the board used to make boxes and cartons in Canada is 100% recycled content.

Canopy also neglects to mention that Canada's overall paper recovery rate is almost 70%, one of the highest rates in the world,[18] and that paper (mainly old corrugated boxes) is the most recycled material in Canada, representing almost 40% of the country's total recycling effort.[19]

It also fails to recognize that paper (mainly old corrugated boxes) is the mainstay of provincial Blue Box programs. Several paper materials (corrugated boxes, magazines, and newspapers) have sent for recycling rates in the high 80s and 90s.[20] In Ontario, most of this recovered paper is supplied to packaging mills that use it to produce new, 100% recycled content boxes and cartons. Ontario thus already has a home-grown circular economy where used paper is recycled over and over again. Canopy wants to scrap this continuous recycling loop in favour of unproven wheat straw?

Canopy does at least acknowledge one key problem with its proposed "alternative" fibres. Mills using agricultural residues will need to be located "near where farmers end up with lots of wheat straw."[21] Well, that's an interesting admission. Considering that most existing and new packaging mills or machines in Canada use recycled content (not virgin fibres), and that they are deliberately built next to the source of those fibres (that is, in towns and cities), why on earth would they relocate to a predominantly rural area to use wheat straw? It does not make any practical or market sense.

All these points have been made to Canopy through blogs and deliberate circulation to Canopy staff and supporters. *But nothing seems to change.*

Canopy continues to flood the marketplace with smears and misinformation about paper packaging while trolling for "alternative fibre" or "next generation" investor support. And if you could send a little money Canopy's way that would be appreciated. In US or Canadian dollars. Either will do.

Is Canopy's wheat straw alternative any better?

Canopy's Nicole Rycroft is reported as saying that Columbia Pulp was a "lightbulb moment" for her about the climate crisis, and that it promised to usher in "a new green resource sector," an alternative world of 200 mills not using trees to make paper.[22] Let's have a closer look at the claims being made for Columbia Pulp.

Claim 1: Agricultural fibre pulp mills (according to Canopy) are using technologies that use less water, chemicals, and energy than conventional wood kraft pulp mills. [23]

Are we comparing like with like here? Because in the case of Columbia Pulp, we are not. Columbia Pulp has far less equipment than a conventional wood-pulp mill, so of course it uses less water, chemicals, and energy. Unlike most pulp mills, even other straw pulp mills, Columbia has no straw-cleaning equipment before its pulping stage; its washing system to remove pulping chemicals is inadequate; and it has no equipment to clean up and reuse its process water.[24]

There are serious consequences for these deliberate design choices: the presence of debris like stones, dirt, metal, and plastic in the straw will damage mill equipment, with sand and dirt possibly ending up in the final pulp itself. Some of the pulping chemicals could end up in the same place; and not drying the pulp (as most pulp mills do) will not only increase transport costs and carbon dioxide emissions, it also means the pulp will go mouldy if not used promptly enough.

Comparing what is basically half a mill with a normal wood-pulp mill (or even a straw-pulp mill) is clearly invalid. And making life-cycle and carbon footprint claims in a nine-page slide presentation on its website doesn't say much except how great Columbia Pulp is, with no back-up information.[25] How about a life-cycle analysis that meets ISO 14040, including a publicly available independent third-party review?

Claim 2: The cost of building a new agricultural pulp mill (according to Canopy) is about $US200 million.[26]

Good luck with that! How about $US375 million, almost double? Columbia Pulp's own documents indicate an initial project cost of $US184 million, which subsequently ballooned to $US285 million, and that includes a lot of reconditioned used equipment from the wood-pulp sector.[27] It would require another $US80 million to $US90 million to add straw-cleaning and proper washing equipment and so on to get the mill up to full production, which means the full cost is getting *close to double* what Canopy is citing to pulp customers and to potential investors.

Market issues

And then there is a whole slew of market issues. Columbia Pulp talks about a "bio-polymer co-product" from the mill. These are fancy words for black liquor, which wood-pulp (and most non-wood pulp) mills produce and recover for energy or convert to a solid for disposal. But because Columbia Pulp has deliberately chosen not to install a full chemical recovery system, it has a huge amount of black liquor (45.2 million gallons a year) that it now has to do something about.[28]

Columbia Pulp intends to sell the black liquor as a liquid bio-polymer, and this is critical to the mill's economic success because it represents about 34% of the mill's total annual revenue.[29] If the co-product markets fail to materialize, however, disposal of the black liquor will become a cost that could drag the mill down.

Has Canopy thought through what 200 of these straw pulp mills it wants investors to build around the world (20 in the United States and 8 in Canada) will do with all this black liquor (about 9 billion gallons of the stuff)? There is a good reason why wood-pulp (and most non-wood pulp) mills have chemical recovery boilers. There are very few markets for black liquor that appear to be environmentally acceptable.[30]

But the major market issue that Columbia Pulp faces stems from the way the mill has been designed. Given the equipment it has chosen not to install, all it can produce is a low-quality short-fibre product that will not recycle as well as wood pulp. It will really struggle to be competitive with longer-fibre wood pulp which has the strength properties required for packaging. And if Columbia Pulp can't sell its product, it's game over.

Canopy may see Columbia Pulp as a "lightbulb moment" on the way to a world of "paper without trees." Seriously, though, it needs to take its blinkers off. Continuing to make false and misleading claims about wood pulp and paper packaging while touting a wheat straw model that clearly has major problems will only further damage its credibility.

Chapter 34
Waste (Definitions)
Lies, damned lies, and statistics

Everyone thinks that they know what waste is. It's what you put out as garbage, right? Not quite. It's a lot broader than that. We also flush *liquid* wastes into the sewers and sewage treatment plants, and allow *energy* waste to escape such as the heat from light bulbs, steam from cooking, warm air through an open door.

Even within categories of waste we have to be very careful how we describe it. When the media talks about North Americans being wasteful, or being "among the world's champion garbage creators,"[1] which part of the waste stream do you think they mean? All of it? Total solid waste? Including tailings from mines? Construction, renovation, and demolition debris? Hazardous waste like paints and solvents, or medical wastes? Are they included? Or maybe they just mean residential or municipal solid waste, or waste from industry, offices, and hospitals?

There is a confusing mix of different terms and definitions of solid waste, for example. And different statistics (and conclusions to be drawn) for every single category of it. And that's not even getting into the widespread confusion over the *generation* of waste or what's called the waste stream, compared to the actual dumping or disposal of waste. Do we measure our wastefulness by what we generate (consume) or by what we actually send to landfill or incineration (disposal)? These are two very different things (see **GENERATION (OF WASTE)**).

It's not as if anyone is deliberately lying here. *Mostly!* It's just that many people do not speak or write as precisely as they should, or are ill-informed, or use statistics incorrectly, or tend to exaggerate depending on their specific agenda or knowledge base. And then there's the "tarred with the same brush" factor. Just because most plastics currently end up as waste doesn't mean that "Recycling is dead" or that most other materials go to waste as well.

Unfortunately, there are no globally accepted definitions of solid waste outlining what counts and what doesn't, so valid and credible comparisons are difficult. The 37-member Organisation for Economic Co-Operation and Development (OECD), for example, regularly reports on waste generation but focuses on the municipal waste stream, which it defines as waste collected and treated by or for municipalities. Privately collected waste is not included in the OECD data. Nor is waste from municipal sewage networks or from construction and demolition activities.[2]

The World Bank released a global review of solid waste management in 2012 and updated it in 2018. At least it attempted to gather data on a broad range of waste streams, but data gathering, interpretation, and making credible comparisons remain a worldwide problem. One recent analysis of this World Bank data had Canadians producing the most solid waste per person in the world, with the United States ranked third. But this was *generation* data, not *disposal* data, and it's questionable whether comparisons that don't take population densities and climate into account are fair ones. Maybe the fairest comparisons are between similar-sized and geographically located cities such as Toronto and Chicago rather than between small and large nations with widely varying population densities.[3]

Global comparisons are one thing. We even have problems comparing solid waste data between the United States and Canada and I don't mean the additional hassle of converting short tons to metric tonnes and vice versa![4] The US EPA, for example, measures *municipal* solid waste that includes packaging, food waste, yard trimmings, furniture, electronics, tires and appliances from residential sources, but also some wastes from commercial and institutional locations such as restaurants, grocery stores, schools, hospitals, and factory cafeterias. But it excludes other industrial process wastes, hazardous waste, and construction and demolition waste.

Canada, on the other hand, divides solid waste by where it comes from (residential and non-residential) sources. And unlike the United States, Canada includes construction, renovation, and demolition debris in the industrial (non-residential) portion of its waste stream.

There's another wrinkle! All these definitions use the weight of material (tons/tonnes) as their unit of measure rather than volume or something else. While measuring by weight is certainly convenient, it tends to distort the overall waste picture. As they say, landfills don't get heavy (through added weight), they get fat (through added volume).

With all that (and the population differences) in mind, here's a snapshot of some of the latest solid waste data from the United States and Canada, with the relevant caveats thrown in.

CANADA

(Latest Statistics Canada data is for calendar year 2018 and is expressed in metric tonnes).

Waste Generation: 35.55 million (metric tonnes). Solid non-hazardous waste from the residential, industrial, commercial, and institutional (IC & I) sectors, including construction and demolition waste.

Waste Diversion : 9.81 million metric tonnes. Includes material sent for recycling and composting but excludes combustion with energy recovery. Some 53% was diverted by the residential sector, 47% by the industrial (IC & I sector).[5] Paper was the single largest material diverted (36%), followed by organics (29%), construction, renovation and demolition debris (7%), and ferrous metals (6%).

Waste Disposal: 25.73 million metric tonnes. This was broken out as 42% coming from residential sources and 58% from non-residential (IC & I) sources.

Further details, including provincial breakouts, are available from various Statistics Canada tables: *Waste materials diverted, by type and by source* Table 38-10-0138-01; and *Disposal of waste, by source* Table 38-10-0032-01.

UNITED STATES

(Latest data from the Environmental Protection Agency is for calendar year 2018 and is expressed in short tons).

Waste Generation: 292.4 million short tons. Measures municipal solid waste, which it defines as residential waste, including waste from multi-family housing, as well as commercial and institutional locations such as businesses, schools, and hospitals. It excludes industrial, hazardous, and construction and demolition wastes.

Waste Diversion: 146.2 million short tons. Includes materials sent for recycling, composting, and for combustion with energy recovery. Most of the diversion came through recycling (47%), followed by combustion with energy recovery (24%) and composting (17%). Paper and paperboard packaging was the major item sent for recycling (67% of all recycling).

Waste Disposal: 146.1 million short tons. Does not include construction and demolition debris.

Further details are available from the EPA report: *Advancing Sustainable Materials Management: 2018 Fact Sheet, December 2020. https://www.epa.gov/sites/default/files/2021-01/documents/2018_ff_fact_sheet_dec_2020_fnl_508.pdf*

See also **GENERATION (OF WASTE), PACKAGING WASTE,** and **RECYCLED.**

Chapter 35

Xmas Paper
The elephant joke that makes you want to cry

My colleague Allen Kirkpatrick came in to my office about three weeks before Christmas 2019 waving a copy of an article that had appeared in his local digital newspaper. "I am gobsmacked by the reference to 540,000 tonnes of wrapping paper going to landfill," he exclaimed. "How could this possibly be? It takes a whole year for a really large packaging mill to produce that kind of tonnage."

So began a strange voyage of discovery. He was right, of course. The number made no sense at all, but there it was in black and white. *Half a million tonnes of wrapping paper ending up in landfill when the total amount used in the country was not even one-tenth of that! Something was definitely wrong with this picture.*

Then, all of a sudden, the number was everywhere. On Global TV, in *The Canadian Press news feeds*, in the *Globe and Mail*. And they all quoted the same number: 540,000 tonnes. "*Picture this: 540,000 tonnes of wrapping paper – the equivalent of the weight of 100,000 elephants or 4.5 CN Towers.*"[1]

As the story spread, so did the confusion. Some media just listed wrapping paper, others added in paper and plastic gift bags. Which was it? And was this *enormous* tonnage just dumped over Christmas (as a couple of stories claimed) or was it the annual *generation* of these materials (what was sold to consumers in the first place)? If the material was landfilled, where did the numbers come from? *This little beauty was getting murkier by the minute.*

The media claimed its source of information was the advocacy group Zero Waste Canada. And on its website were more claims: "Each Canadian tosses 50 kilograms of garbage over the Christmas holiday, 25% more than the rest of the year thanks to the purchase of 3,000 tonnes of foil, 2.6 billion Christmas cards, and six million rolls of tape. Altogether, 540,000 tonnes of wrapping paper and gift bags are thrown out a year."

Okay, so we're talking about a lot more than just wrapping paper then. And we're not talking about Christmas alone, we're talking about what's thrown out over a 12-month period. *Glad we cleared up some of that because the media was giving different versions of what the 540,000 tonnes was -- or wasn't.*

I now tried to get a full copy of what the media was referring to as a "2017 study" so that I could look at the numbers behind the numbers. But Zero Waste Canada was not returning my calls or emails. I emailed the writer of the *Globe and Mail* article. No, she didn't have the full report either, but had got the numbers from Zero Waste Canada.

Then Barb Hetherington of Zero Waste Canada responded with some surprising news. No, her organization had not, in fact, sent out any press releases on this subject. Nor was it a "report" as some news articles were portraying it. What was happening now, she wrote, had just seemed "to morph over (the) news services." In fact, she said, the information the media were now quoting had been used in a Christmas blog that had been written several years ago, with the original statistics coming from the Recycling Council of British Columbia (RCBC).

What? Several years ago? There was no *actual Zero Waste Canada study then? The media was quoting numbers from a study that didn't exist?* This story was getting stranger by the minute, with still no clear picture of where the original information had come from.

I tracked down the RCBC press release and found the claim: "The annual waste generation in Canada from gift-wrapping and shopping bags equals about 545,000 tonnes." But, unfortunately, no source was given for this information and it implied *generation* (what's produced for sale in the marketplace, not what ends up being trashed, which can be something quite different. See **GENERATION (OF WASTE)**. But check the date. This press release using the 545,000 tonnes number was December 5, 2007, a full *12 years before* the latest media circus![2] *What was going on here?*

"That's definitely a flash from the past," the Recycling Council's Harvinder Aujala told me. "I don't have the source for that specific statistic. For some statistics where Canadian data is not available, we may extrapolate from US numbers. For example, we are roughly 10% of the population, so take the US number and use a 10% value. I'm not certain if that is what was done in this instance, but it may explain why you may not be able to find a similar Canadian data source. If you do find the source, please feel free to share. We've stopped using it in our outreach since we can't authenticate the number."

Thanks a bunch, I responded. This was like a mystery tour. People were still quoting the number but no one knew where it came from! "I know!" Aujala agreed. "That's why we stopped using it. We need Nancy Drew on the case ☺."

I was no Nancy but I did manage to track down the author of the RCBC press release. Unfortunately, Mairi Welman could tell me nothing. "No idea. That was 13 years ago." *You're not kidding!*[3]

Aujala had given me a clue though, to check out an *even earlier* publication of the Regional District of Nanaimo. And there I found yet another claim using exactly the same number, although it was ambiguous about whether this was material for sale or waste actually dumped: "In Canada, the annual waste from gift wrapping and shopping bags equals about 545,000 tonnes." But again, no source for the information. And guess what? This item was published in 2002. *Yes, a full 17 years before its current incarnation!*

Your intrepid and now rather tired investigator then touched base with the Regional District of Nanaimo, only to be told that it couldn't confirm where the data had come from "as the staff member is no longer with us."[4] *Ha! Why was I not surprised after 17 years!*

At this point, I finally gave up. I no longer had the time or the patience to investigate any further. The claim and its comparison to the weight of 100,000 elephants was clearly suspect. Whether it included wrapping paper or other stuff was unclear. If it was material sold to consumers or sent to landfill, uncertain. Where the actual data came from, unknown. And the clincher, whatever the "story" was, it seemed to be at least 17 years old!

Why hadn't the media checked out the "study" for themselves instead of just grabbing for an easy headline (the elephants)? Everyone had reported this as a 2017 study by Zero Waste Canada. In fact, there had been no such study. What the media were instead quoting were estimates of either what was placed in the marketplace or what was landfilled (it was not entirely clear) of more than just wrapping paper, by persons unknown, way back in 2002. This whole sorry episode raises serious questions about how people access information and report on it. It does not make journalists look good. But it's great for the purveyors of little green lies and BS.

Postscript: In sharing this story with an industry expert, we suspect that person(s) unknown saw some statistics from the Pulp and Paper Products Council indicating that 545,000 tonnes of "Wrapping Paper" were consumed in Canada back in 2002 and jumped to a false conclusion.

In fact, the "Wrapping Paper" that the council was talking about was wrapping paper sold to customers (not landfilled) and it included all multiwall sacks and bags produced to hold flour, cement, pet food, and other food wrapping.

If our suspicion is right, this would explain the high number (the 545,000). But it certainly doesn't explain how the media handled this information back in 2002 and then somehow regurgitated (and mangled it) some 17 years later!

See also **GENERATION (OF WASTE)**.

Chapter 36

"Zero" Waste

Sounds good, but is it for real?

We are surrounded by zeroes. Zero carbon, zero net carbon, zero emissions.[1] And then there's zero waste.

What does it actually mean? Does it mean "absolutely no waste"? Nothing? Not a piece? If I wore a hat, I would take it off to the people you occasionally see in the media who claim to have gone garbage-free for weeks, or months, or longer. Bravo! But what do you do with household waste like lint from the dryer, soiled tissues, ballpoint pens, chewing gum? I guess one answer would be not to use them in the first place.

That's the approach of the Ellen MacArthur Foundation (EMF). Waste is to be "designed out." It is not an option. Products and packaging should be designed for reuse, remanufacture, and recycling so they endlessly circulate in the economy. Disposal is therefore not needed because no waste is generated.

Okay, but what do you do about toilet paper? Just because you flush it does not mean it wasn't generated as waste! The closest that the foundation comes to mentioning waste is a reference to "leakage" that must be minimized.[2]

Some people say that if Nature can do it, then we can do it. It's a nice thought, but a tad unrealistic. Because Nature is not zero waste. Sure, everything feeds on everything else, but there is always left-over waste. As a colleague recently pointed out to me, the dinosaurs might have disappeared but their waste (their calcified bones) is still around some 65 million years later.

So, the first thing to understand about zero waste is that it's not really zero. It's more like a *concept* or an *aspirational goal*. The Zero Waste International Alliance calls it "a philosophy, a strategy, and a set of practical tools seeking to eliminate waste, not manage it."[3] Zero Waste Europe describes it as "a goal that is ethical, economical, efficient and visionary, to guide people in changing their lifestyles and practices to emulate sustainable natural cycles, where all discarded materials are designed to become resources for others to use."[4]

This sounds like an eminently reasonable wish-for. In Canada, the federal and provincial ministers of the environment (the Canadian Council of Ministers for the Environment or CCME) have come up with a Zero Plastic Waste Action Plan, "an action plan that targets zero waste [but] does not mean zero plastic. It means plastic reduction and improved plastics life-cycle management to achieve a more circular plastics economy."[5]

Okay, so it's a *target*. And in the United States, the Conference of Mayors has adopted a definition of *zero waste* and a set of zero waste principles that recognizes a hierarchy of material management, from product redesign down to landfill disposal.

All these definitions and action plans are basically strategies to *reduce waste going to landfill*. Where they differ is on the relative emphasis they place on parts of that strategy and how they measure it. The Zero Waste International Alliance, for example, does not consider any heat-based waste management system (energy-from-waste, gasification, pyrolysis) to be part of a zero-waste strategy, even if burning waste instead of coal (fuel substitution) is a better environmental alternative.

So, when you hear companies embracing and committing to zero-waste goals, it's a good idea to clarify whether they mean completely eliminating the production of items that currently mostly go to waste; or improving their production processes ("designing out" waste so that products can be constantly reused, remanufactured, recycled); or whether they mean zero (physical) waste will be sent to landfill from their facilities. There's a world of difference, and the devil is *always* in the details.

Chapter 37

Conclusion
Reflections on some turds and apple pie

When I started out on this "little project" a few months ago, I knew it would be a stiff challenge. Not that there's a shortage of false and misleading claims or exaggerations, omissions, lies, spin, smear campaigns, and straight-out hypocrisy. Far from it. And that's just in *my* area of work experience: the paper, packaging, recycling, and waste industries.

The challenge was in actually nailing down the little green lies and the BS because sometimes they are obscured, and there are often different ways of looking at issues. Sometimes the "lies" aren't even lies. For example, I have included some urban myths about cardboard, pizza boxes, pristine forest, about what's actually being recycled, and waste generation, more for educational reasons than for any other. Because a lot of us (myself included) often don't really know what we are talking about, although that doesn't seem to stop us from sounding off occasionally!

Many of the so-called green lies outlined here are about the meaning of words or definitions, or the context in which a phrase or expression is used. For example, how do you define a *degraded* forest? What does *recyclable* mean? Is *zero waste* for real? What about *killing* and *saving* trees?

There are also what I will politely call "inadvertent" lies, and lies arising from ignorance. Then there are the more deliberate attempts to mislead, obscure, exaggerate, or smear. I have tried to outline these as objectively as I can, using available facts and their accompanying sources in the endnotes. If it's not accurate, I want to know about it.

Some people will not be pleased with what I have written. And some, no doubt, will seek to dismiss me as just some former paper industry hack. To them, I would suggest that they look at my environmental track record, and then "play the ball, not the man" (to use an old rugby expression). That is, challenge the information on its accuracy, rather than the messenger who delivered it.

Words *do* matter, and it's important that they are based on fact, not fiction. There is a clear need to broaden our understanding of environmental issues, to take all the facts into account, and not just to promote the information we like, or that which fits our particular world-view. Because there are consequences for telling little green lies: flawed government policies, misguided corporate commitments, the hardening of positions, delays in needed action.

I am hopeful because there seems to be a growing groundswell against greenwashing in general. Governments and the financial community finally seem to be waking up. The danger, of course, is that these action plans and commitments and vision statements will just end up as more words and empty promises.

The environmental, social, and governance (ESG) community needs to ensure that they don't, that it doesn't become just another forum for talk, talk, talk and a green rubber stamp for smooth marketers. Environmental groups who expect and demand that government and industry be transparent and accountable need to ditch the little green halos and recognize that they too need to be transparent and accountable. Credibility is earned; it's not a right.

In all this, the media plays a key role. As a former journalist myself, I understand the pressure of deadlines and competition. But when you receive information from a government, from industry, or from an environmental group, please do not swallow the apple pie without having a good look at it first. The **XMAS PAPER** entry is an appalling example of sloppy journalism.

The media plays such an important role in education. And consumers, unfortunately, are not very ecologically literate. That may sound harsh (arrogant, even) but I think it's true. And the media is crucial in removing and reducing that ignorance, in challenging the assumptions behind many environmental claims, and in exposing the frauds and the cons as publicly as possible.

Because that's our best hope. Enforcement by governments, by regulations, by guidelines, is basically a complaint-driven process. And if consumers don't know enough about an issue through the media, or how to channel their complaints, then effectively there is no enforcement. And we all know what that means. More turds and apple pie.

ACKNOWLEDGEMENTS

In an effort like this there are many unseen contributors, individuals who wish to remain anonymous for personal, business, or public policy reasons. I thank them sincerely, especially the folks at the Canadian Forest Service and the Forest Products Association of Canada for their technical input and advice on key forest-related issues.

There are others who helped in a variety of different ways, big and small, who I also wish to acknowledge (in alphabetical order): Catherine Ashworth, Martin Fairbanks, Martine Hamel, Jenny Hillard, Bob Hurter, Lynn Johannson, Pat Kane, Dan Lantz, Louis Lemaire, David McDonald, Theo Mullinder (of "apple pie" fame), Paul Palmer-Edwards, Kathie Rowzi, Heather Sangster, and Doug Symington. Thank you one and all.

KEY SOURCES

Environmental labelling and advertising
International Organization for Standardization (ISO),

https://www.iso.org/standard/66652.html.

Competition Bureau Canada, *Environmental Claims: A Guide for Industry and Advertisers,* June 2008. https://www.competitionbureau.gc.ca/eic/site/cb-bc.nsf/eng/04607.html

US Federal Trade Commission (FTC), "260.2 Interpretation of Environmental Marketing Claims," *Green Guides (Revised),* October 1, 2012,

https://www.ftc.gov/sites/default/files/attachments/press-releases/ftc-issues-revised-green-guides/greenguides.pdf

Forestry
"8 Facts About Canada's Boreal Forest," Natural Resources Canada, n.d., https://www.nrcan.gc.ca/our-natural-resources/forests-forestry/sustainable-forest-management/boreal-forest/8-facts-about-canadas-boreal-forest/17394

Certification Canada www.certificationcanada.org/en/statistics/canadian-statistics/

Food and Agricultural Organization of the United Nations (FAO) and UN Environment Programme (UNEP), *The State of the World's Forests 2020: Forests, Biodiversity and People,* 2020, https://www.fao.org/3/ca8642en/ca8642en.pdf.

Food and Agricultural Organization of the United Nations (FAO), *Global Forest Resources Assessment 2020: Country Reports*, 2020, www.fao.org/forest-resources-assessment/fra-2020/country-reports/en/.

Food and Agricultural Organization of the United Nations (FAO), *Global Forest Resources Assessment 2020: Key Findings*, 2020, https://www.fao.org/3/ca8753en/CA8753EN.pdf.

Food and Agricultural Organization of the United Nations (FAO), *Global Forest Resources Assessment (2020): Main Report*, 2020, https://www.fao.org/3/ca9825en/ca9825en.pdf.

Food and Agricultural Organization of the United Nations (FAO), *Global Forest Resources Assessment (2020) Terms and Definitions* (working paper 188) 2018, https://www.fao.org/3/i8661en/i8661en.pdf.

National Forestry Inventory (Canada) https://ca.nfis.org/index_eng.html

Natural Resources Canada (NRC), The State of Canada's Forests: Annual Report 2020, 2020, https://www.nrcan.gc.ca/our-natural-resources/forests-forestry/state-canadas-forests-report/16496.

Sonja N. Oswalt et al., Forest Resources of the United States, 2017, A Technical Document Supporting the Forest Service 2020 RPA Assessment (Gen. Tech. Report WO-97), US Department of Agriculture Forest Service, March 2019, https://www.fs.fed.us/research/publications/gtr/gtr_wo97.pdf.

Waste

Statistics Canada, https://www.150.statcan.gc.ca/n1/en/surveys/2009 .

US Environmental Protection Agency (EPA), *Advancing Sustainable Materials Management: 2018 Fact Sheet*, December 2020, www.epa.gov/sites/production/files/2021-01/documents/2018_ff_fact_sheet_dec_2020_fnl_508.pdf.

Organization for Economic Development and Cooperation (OECD), https://oecd.org/.

Silpa Kaza *et al.*, What a Waste 2.0: A Global Snapshot of Solid Waste Management to 2050, Urban Development, Washington, DC, World Bank. © World Bank, 2018, https://openknowledge.worldbank.org/handle/10986/30317; and Daniel Hoornweg and Perinaz Bhada-Tata, *What a Waste: A Global Review of Solid Waste Management* (Urban development series; knowledge papers no. 15), World Bank, Washington, DC, © World Bank, 2012, https://openknowledge.worldbank.org/handle/10986/17388.

APPENDIX 1

1. National Deforestation Rates

Notes to the Data:

The source for this data is the 236 country reports[1] supplied to the Food and Agriculture Organization of the United Nations (FAO) in preparation for its latest *Global Forest Resources Assessment 2020*.[2] Prior to collating all this information, FAO staff and independent forestry experts review the data supplied by different countries to ensure it is as accurate as possible. Even so, data quality varies. Some are just an expert (desk) assessment (called Tier 1). In other cases, data exits but pieces are missing and the data is older (Tier 2). The best data (Tier 3) is highly reliable, recent, and national.

The table that follows is derived from two questions the FAO asked the participating countries as it compiled its 2020 assessment. The first question related to the forest area of a country (Question 1b), and the second question to deforestation (Question 1d). In both cases, FAO definitions of forest area and deforestation were used, as per the FAO's *Terms and Definitions*.[3]

For example, Canada's forest area in 2020 was estimated to be 346,928,100 hectares (Question 1b) and its deforestation to be 37,520 hectares (Question 1d). The deforestation hectares were then simply divided by the forest hectares to get the percentage of forest area that was deforested (averaged over the five-year period 2015 to 2020). In Canada's case, 37,520 hectares of 346.9 million hectares equals 0.01%. The same process was applied to all 236 country reports.

---

1   FAO, *Global Forest Resources Assessment 2020: Country Reports*, 2020, www.fao.org/forest-resources-assessment/fra-2020/country-reports/en/.
2   FAO, 2020. *Global Forest Resources Assessment 2020, Main Report*, 2020, www.fao.org/documents/card/en/c/ca9825en.
3   FAO, *Global Forest Resources Assessment 2020: Terms and Definitions (working paper 188)*, 2018, p.8, https://www.fao.org/3/I8661EN/i8661en.pdf.

The FAO notes that while the quality of deforestation data supplied by individual countries is good and higher than in previous assessments, major gaps and deficiencies remain. The FAO was specifically asked to comment on the approach taken to produce this table and whether it would like to add any further caveats to its interpretation. The results for Mauritania and Azerbaijan, for example, seem entirely out of sync with other countries. At the time of writing, no response from FAO had been received.

| National Deforestation Rates ||
| Over 1% ||
Country	% Forest Land Deforested
Mauritania	14.5
Azerbaijan	7.6
Liechtenstein	3.1
Nicaragua	3.1
Djibouti	2.8
Uganda	2.2
Malawi	1.9
Cabo Verde	1.8
Paraguay	1.7
Singapore	1.5
Montenegro	1.5
Sudan	1.4
Niger	1.4
Central African Republic	1.3
Somalia	1.3
Sao Tome	1.2
South Africa	1.2

National Deforestation Rates	
Over 1%	
Country	% Forest Land Deforested
Tanzania	1.0
Myanmar	1.0

National Deforestation Rates	
Less than 1%	
Country	% Forest Land Deforested
India	0.9
Belize	0.9
El Salvador	0.8
Nigeria	0.8
Mozambique	0.7
Indonesia	0.7
Ecuador	0.7
Senegal	0.6
Netherlands	0.6
Ethiopia	0.5
Switzerland	0.5
Bolivia	0.5
Argentina	0.5
Mayotte	0.4
Zambia	0.4
Togo	0.4
Liberia	0.4

National Deforestation Rates	
Less than 1%	
Country	% Forest Land Deforested
Korea (DPR) North	0.4
Uzbekistan	0.4
Honduras	0.4
Guadeloupe	0.3
Brazil	0.3
Equatorial Guinea	0.3
Colombia	0.3
Guatemala	0.3
Mauritius	0.3
Martinique	0.3
Panama	0.3
Cameroon	0.3
Algeria	0.3
Zimbabwe	0.3
Mexico	0.3
Peru	0.2
Venezuela	0.2
Belgium	0.2
Estonia	0.2
Thailand	0.2
Slovenia	0.2
Korea Rep. (South)	0.2
Hungary	0.2
Austria	0.2

National Deforestation Rates	
Less than 1%	
Country	% Forest Land Deforested
Denmark	0.1
Papua New Guinea	0.1
Jamaica	0.1
Moldova	0.1
Gabon	0.1
Tunisia	0.1
Ireland	0.1
Suriname	0.1
French Guinea	0.1
New Zealand	0.1
Congo	0.1
Germany	0.1
China	0.1
Chile	0.1
Guyana	0.1

National Deforestation Rates	
Less than half of 1%	
Country	% Forest Land Deforested
Norway	0.05
Sweden	0.05
Belarus	0.04
Spain	0.02
Bhutan	0.02

National Deforestation Rates	
Less than half of 1%	
Country	% Forest Land Deforested
Vietnam	0.01
Mongolia	0.01
Latvia	0.01
CANADA	0.01
Poland	0.01
Lithuania	0.01
Turkey	0.01
Croatia	0.01
Serbia	0.01
Ukraine	0.01
Romania	0.01

ENDNOTES

Every effort has been made to include accurate and current references in the Endnotes. Some of the URLs may have been changed or removed after the publication date.

"ANCIENT" FORESTS

1   See **FOREST**. A primary forest is defined by the Food and Agriculture Organization of the United Nations (FAO) as a "naturally regenerated forest of native tree species, where there are no clearly visible indications of human activities and the ecological processes are not significantly disturbed." (FAO, *Global Forest Resources Assessment 2020 Terms and Definitions* (working paper 188, 2018, p.8. https://www.fao.org/3/I8661EN/i8661en.pdf).

In the explanatory notes, the FAO adds that primary forest "includes both pristine and managed forests" that meet the definition; includes forests where Indigenous peoples engage in traditional forest stewardship activities that meet the definition; includes forest with visible signs of abiotic damage (such as storm, snow, drought, fire) and biotic damage (such as insects, pests, and diseases); but excludes forests where hunting, poaching, trapping or gathering have caused significant native species loss or disturbance to ecological processes. Some key characteristics of primary forests are that they show natural forest dynamics such as natural tree species composition; the occurrence of dead wood, natural age structure, and natural regenerative processes; encompass an area large enough to maintain their natural ecological processes; and indicate no known significant human intervention or the last significant human intervention was long enough ago to have allowed the natural species composition and processes to have become re-established (Ibid.).

2   *Roadmap to Recovery: The World's Last Intact Forest Landscapes,* Greenpeace, 2006. https://www.greenpeace.org/usa/research/roadmap-to-recovery-the-world/.

3   Kate Goldblum, "What is the oldest tree in the world?" '*Live Science* online, August 23, 2016. https://www.livescience.com/29152-oldest-tree-in-the-world.html

4   *Is Canada's Boreal Forest Ancient?* Canadian Forest Service, Natural Resources Canada, September 2009. http://cfs.nrcan.gc.ca/pubware-house/pdfs/30085.pdf

5   National Forest Inventory, (Canada) *Table 14.0 Area (1000 ha) of forest land by species group, and age class in Canada,* December 2013. https://nfi.org/resources/general/summaries/t0/en/CA_T14_LSAGE20_AREA_en.pdf

6   Only 1% of Canada's boreal is more than 200 years old. National Forest Inventory (Canada) *Table 5.2 Area (1000 ha) of forest land by forest type, age class and boreal zone in Canada,* December 2013. https://nfi.org/resources/general/summaries/t0/en/BORE/pdf/BORE_T5_FORAGE20_AREA_en.pdf

7   *Is Canada's Boreal Forest Ancient?* Ibid.

8   "How We Protect Forests," Canopy www.canopyplanet.org/campaigns/protecting-forests; "Ancient and Endangered Forests Defined," Canopy, www.canopyplanet.org/wp-content/uploads/2015/03/AncientandEndangeredForestsDefined.pdf; "Endangered Forests: Priority High Conservation Value Forests For Protection Guidance For Corporate Commitments," Canopy/*Wye Group Report* April 25-27, 2002, www.canopyplanet.org/wp-content/uploads/2015/03/Wye-EF-Report.pdf (all accessed 15 August, 2021). Contributing organizations to the report included World Resources Institute, World Wildlife Fund-US, Natural Resources Defense Council, Rainforest Action Network, ForestEthics, and Greenpeace.

9   Dr. James (Jim) Strittholt, Conservation Biology Institute. For example, in his paper abstract "Primary and Intact Rainforest Assessment and Protection Campaign, British Columbia, Canada." Projects June 2018 to December 2019, https://consbio.org/products/projects/rainforest-protection-british-columbia-canada.

10 The only scientific back-up that Canopy offers relates to endangered forests (the *Wye Group Report*, see endnote 8). No specific scientific evidence is offered for "ancient" forests. There are other problems with the Ancient Forest Friendly brand (www.canopyplanet.org/resources/elements-of-a-leading-policy/ (accessed August 15, 2021). It promotes only one certifier of sustainable forestry (the Forest Stewardship Council, FSC) even though the discussion document "Endangered Forests" held out the possibility that "equivalent, certified sustainable forestry operations" might be included. Canadian Forestry ministers have approved three third-party certifiers (including FSC) as being "consistent with national and international agreements related to sustainable forest management and meeting criteria for balancing interests, being objective and science-based, (and being) implementable and practical." Canopy also promotes post-consumer recycled content over pre-consumer recycled content (see **RECYCLED CONTENT**), alternative fibres (see **SUGARCANE** (**BAGASSE**)), and a questionable wheat straw model (see **"TREE-FREE."**).

11 Valerie Langer, "What's in the Box? Part 1," Canopy, November 6, 2019. https://canopyplanet.org/whats-in-the-box-part-1/.

12 See Suzanne Simard, *Finding the Mother Tree* (Toronto: Allen Lane, 2021).

13 "[Oceans] provide rich, complex ecosystems for marine life that also provide billions of people with food and livelihoods," Laura Repas, "Single Use to Systems Change," Canopy, February 16, 2021. https://canopyplanet.org/single-use-to-systems-change/.

14 Jennifer Skene (with Shelley Vinyard),*The Issue with Tissue*, Natural Resources Defense Council and STAND.earth, February 2019, https://www.stand.earth/sites/default/files/StandEarth-NRDC-IssueWithTissue-Report.pdf (see **TOILET PAPER**); and Heather Reisman (see John Mullinder, "Reisman Reveals Woeful Ignorance of Forest and Paper Issues," johnmullinder.ca, April 18, 2021 https://johnmullinder.ca/reisman-reveals-woeful-ignorance-of-forest-and-paper-issues/.

15 Pack4Good campaign "Did you Know," Canopy, n.d., https://canopyplanet.org/campaigns/pack4good/; and Laura Repas, "188 global groups say it's time to 'make the

throw-away go away'," February 16, 2021. https://canopyplanet.org/188-global-groups-say-its-time-to-make-the-throw-away-go-away/, See **"TREE-FREE."**

16   Jennifer Ellen Good and Elin Kelsey, "Is There an 800-Year-Old Tree in Your Toilet Paper?" *Globe and Mail*, May 25, 2021, https://www.theglobeandmail.com/opinion/article-is-there-an-800-year-old-tree-in-your-toilet-paper-the-case-for-an-old/ . See **TOILET PAPER.**

BOREAL FOREST

1   "Aurora," Wikipedia, https://en.wikipedia.org/wiki/Aurora accessed October 8, 2021

2   For those not familiar with Toronto, Steeles Avenue runs across the northern edge of the city and Barrie is a city about 45-minutes drive north of that. In fact, the southernmost edge of the boreal in Ontario is probably around Sudbury, farther north.

3   FAO, *Global Forest Resources Assessment (2020): Main Report 2020*. https://www.fao.org/3/ca9825en/ca9825en.pdf.

4   "8 Facts About Canada's Boreal Forest," Natural Resources Canada, n.d., www.nrcan.gc.ca/our-natural-resources/forests-forestry/sustainable-forest-management/boreal-forest/8-facts-about-canadas-boreal-forest/17394.

5   National Forestry Inventory (Canada), *Table 1.2 Area (1000 ha) of land cover by boreal zone in Canada*, December 2013. https://nfi.nfis.org/resources/general/summaries/t0en/BORE_T4_FOR_AREA_en.pdf

6   Canadian Forest Service analysis covering the years 2000 to 2015 quoted in John Mullinder, "Suzuki Dead Wrong on Paper's Circular Economy," johnmullinder.ca, October 1, 2020, https://johnmullinder.ca/suzuki-dead-wrong-on-papers-circular-economy.

7   Jennifer Skene (with Shelley Vinyard), *The Issue with Tissue*, Natural Resources Defense Council and STAND.earth, February 2019, p.4. https://www.stand.earth/sites/default/files/StandEarth-NRDC-IssueWithTissue-Report.pdf. Skene also talks about corporations coming in "and ravaging large swaths of boreal forest," in an NRDC blog "The Log Con: What's Really Going on In Canada's Forests," July 9, 2019.

8   David Suzuki (with Rachel Plotkin), "Circular Economy Is Too Important to Be Co-opted by Industry," David Suzuki Foundation, August 10, 2020. Suzuki refers to "vast amounts of boreal forest pulped for toilet paper."

CARDBOARD

1   Updated from John Mullinder "What Do You Mean 'Cardboard' Doesn't Exist?" PPEC, September 27, 2013 (Reprinted 2018 in Packaging and the Environment, https://johnmullinder.ca/wp-content/uploads/2018/12/Book-of-Blogs_July 27-2.pdf. Several different terms describe boxes internationally, from *boxes* to *boxboard, paperboard, folding cartons, cartons*, and *cardboard* (sometimes shortened to *card*). In North America, the most common industry terms are *corrugated* and *boxboard* or *paperboard*.

DEFORESTATION

1 FAO, *Global Forest Resources Assessment 2020, Report Canada*, 2020, https:// www.fao.org/3/ca9983en/ca9983en.pdf. Canada reported an imputed deforestation area of 37,520 hectares of an estimated 346,928,100 hectares of forest land for the period 2015 to 2020 (0.0108%). This 0.01% rate places it among the lowest in the world (see **APPENDIX 1: National Deforestation Rates**).

2 For example, photographs taken before and after a strong earthquake in the Costa Rica tropical rainforest in 2009 elicited different responses from forestry experts. To some, the land cover was now bare and therefore had been deforested. Others, favouring the land-use approach, maintained that the area was still forest land (and had therefore not been deforested). H. Gyde Lund, "What is a Degraded Forest?" (white paper on forest degradation definitions prepared for FAO), Forest Information Services, Gainesville, VA, January 11, 2009, https://www.researchgate.net/profile/Gyde.Lund/publications/280921178 What_is_a_degraded_forest/links/55cb3b4d08aebc967dfcadb2/What-is-a-degraded-forest.

3 The definition of *forest* that Canada uses is slightly different to the FAO definition so as to harmonize with the definitions found in the Marrakesh Accords of the United Nations Convention on Climate Change. The Department of Natural Resources Canada -- Canadian Forest Services' National Deforestation Monitoring System and the National Forest Carbon Monitoring, Accounting and Reporting System both define forest as a minimum land area of 1 hectare, with tree crown cover of more than 25%, and with trees having the potential to reach a minimum height of 5 metres at maturity in situ (Andrew Dyk, Don Leckie, Sally Tinis, and Stephanie Ortlepp, *Canada's National Deforestation Monitoring System: System Description*, Canadian Forest Service /Pacific Forestry Centre Information Report BC-X-439, 2015, https://cfs.nrcan.gc.ca/pubwarehouse/pdfs/36042.pdf.

4 FAO, *Global Forest Resources Assessment 2020, Main Report*, 2020, p.18. https://www.fao.org/3/ca9825en/ca9825en.pdf

5 Ibid., *Table 9 Deforestation rate, by climatic domain, for four periods spanning 1990-2020*, p.19. The tropical domain was responsible for 9.3 million hectares/year of deforestation between 2015 and 2020; the subtropical domain 0.5 million hectares/year; the temperate domain 0.31 million hectares/year; and the boreal domain 0.06 million hectares/year.

6 Ibid., *Table 10 Deforestation rate, by region and subregion, for four periods spanning 1990-2020*, p. 19. Africa was responsible for 4.4 million hectares of deforestation/year between 2015 and 2020; South America 2.9 million hectares/year; Asia 2.2 million hectares/year; North and Central America 436,000 hectares/year; Europe 69,000 hectares/year; and Oceania 42,000 hectares/year.

7 Ibid., p.19.

8 FAO, *Global Forest Resources Assessment 2020, Report, United States of America* 2020, https://www.fao.org/3/cb0086en/cb0086en.pdf.

9 Canada's *National Inventory Report 2021* to the United Nations indicates deforestation in 2019 of 49,000 hectares. Settlements include forestry roads, mining, oil and gas developments, hydro infrastructure, transport links and built-up lands. (*National Inventory*

Report 1990-2019: Greenhouse Gas Sources and Sinks in Canada: Part 1, (submission to the United Nations Framework Convention on Climate Change, Ministry of Environment and Climate Change Canada, April 2021, p.172, www.unfccc.int/documents/271493).

10   While conversion of forest land to hydro-electric development was responsible for only 2% of Canada's overall deforestation total in 2018 (Natural Resources Canada, *The State of Canada's Forests: Annual Report 2020*), https://www.nrcan.gc.ca/our-natural-resources/forests-forestry/state-canadas-forests-report/16496, in some years it has been far higher. Some 35,000 hectares of forest was submerged in 1993 when Hydro-Quebec's Laforge-1 reservoir was commissioned, and another 28,000 hectares submerged in 2006 when the Eastmain-1 reservoir came on line (John Mullinder, *Deforestation in Canada and Other Fake News*, (Victoria, BC: Tellwell Talent, 2018). British Columbia's more recent Site C hydro development and the Muskrat Falls project in Labrador will impact Canada's deforestation total in future years.

11   Jim Penman *et al.* (eds.) *IPCC Good Practice Guidance for Land Use, Land-Use Change and Forestry*, IPCC National Greenhouse Gas Inventories Programme/IPCC, 2003, https://www.ipcc.ch/publication/good-practice-guidance-for-land-use-land-use-change-and-forestry/. Each country selects its own minimum size of forest area to measure.

12   John Mullinder, "False Claims and Sloppy Journalism Add to the Public Confusion About Deforestation in Canada," PPEC, January 13, 2020 (Reposted johnmullinder.ca, January 16, 2020, https://www.johnmullinder.ca/false-claims-and-sloppy-journalism-add-to-public-confusion-about-deforestation-in-canada/)

"DEGRADED" FOREST

1   Fragmentation is described by the UN as the division of continuous habitat into smaller and more isolated fragments by both natural and anthropogenic (human) factors. It affects biodiversity and ecosystem processes (FAO and UNEP, *The State of the World's Forests 2020: Forests, Biodiversity and People*, 2020. https://www.fao.org/3/ca8642en/ca8642en.pdf). The least fragmented and most intact forest ecosystems in the world are tropical rainforests and boreal coniferous forest. More than 90% of the forest area in these zones is in patches larger than 1million hectares, much larger than the global average. Often these areas are difficult to access and have low population density. "In the boreal coniferous forest biome, 11% percent of the forest area is in the intact class, mainly in Canada and the Russian Federation. Boreal forest fragmentation is mainly linked to natural disturbances (fire and insect outbreaks). Increased severity of boreal-zone wildfires related to global warming (Walker *et al.*, 2019) might increase fragmentation in the long term." (ibid., p.31). "Forest fragmentation in the boreal tundra woodlands is primarily a consequence of natural conditions and disturbances (climate, wildfire and pests)." (ibid., p.32).

2   H. Gyde Lund, "What Is a Degraded Forest?" (white paper on forest degradation definitions prepared for the FAO), Forest Information Services, Gainesville, VA, January 11, 2009, https://www.researchgate.net/profile/Gyde.Lund/publication/280921178_What_is_a_degraded_forest/links/55cb3b4d08aebc967dfcadb2/What-is-a-degraded-forest.

3   Question 5c in the FAO's *Global Forest Resources Assessment 2020* questionnaire. The 236 country reports are available at https://www.fao.org/forest-resources-assessment/fra-2020/country-reports/en/.

4   Some countries also offered comments. Germany, for example, said there was no special monitoring of forest degradation "because there is no necessity." (FAO, *Global Forest Resources Assessment 2020: Report Germany*, 2020, p.59, https://www.fao.org/3/ca9997en/ca9997en.pdf). Denmark said, "Based on the past 200 years of forest history one may, depending on point of view, argue that all Danish forests are degraded, or the opposite." (FAO, *Global Forest Resources Assessment 2020, Report Denmark*, 2020, p.70, https://www.fao.org/3/ca9987en/ca9987en.pdf.

5   The following countries of the Montreal Process represent 83% of the world's temperate and boreal forests, 49% of all forests, 60% of planted forests, 45% of global roundwood production, and 33% of the world's population (Argentina, Australia, Canada, Chile, China, Japan, Republic of Korea, Mexico, New Zealand, Russian Federation, United States of America, and Uruguay. fs.fed.us/research/sustain/docs/montreal-process/2009-criteria-indicators.pdf.

ENVIRONMENTALLY FRIENDLY, ECO-FRIENDLY

1   US Federal Trade Commission, "260.2 Interpretation and Substantiation of Environmental Marketing Claims," *Green Guides (Revised)*, October 1, 2012, https://www.ftc.gov/sites/default/files/attachments/press-releases/ftc-issues-revised-green-guides/greenguides.pdf.

2   Competition Bureau Canada, *Environmental Claims: A Guide for Industry and Advertisers*, June 2008, https://www.competitionbureau.gc.ca/eic/site/cb-bc.nsf/vwapi/guide-for-industry-and-advertisers-en.pdf/SFILE/guide-for-industry-and-advertisers-en.pdf.

EXAGGERATION

1   Tony Rotherham and John Burrows, "Improvement in Efficiency of Fibre Utilization by the Canadian Forest Products Industry 1970 to 2010," *The Forestry Chronicle* 90, no.66 (2014), https://www.pubs.cif-ifc.orgdoi/10.5558/tfc2014-153

2   World Business Council for Sustainable Development, *Facts & Trends: Fresh & Recycled Fiber Complementarity* (April 12, 2015), https://www.wbcsd.org/Sector-Projects/Forest-Solutions-Group/Resources/Facts-Trends-Fresh-Recycled-Fiber-Complementarity-. The US recycling rate for paper and paperboard was 68.2% in 2018, according to the US EPA *Advancing Sustainable Materials Management 2018 Fact Sheet*, Table 1, p.4. The corrugated box rate was 96.5%, Figure 9, p.10.   www.epa.gov/sites/default/files/2021-01/documents/2018_ff_fact_sheet_dec_2020_fnl_508.pdf

3   Statistics Canada, *Table 38-10-10-0034-01, Materials diverted, by type, inactive*, released February 16, 2021. https://www.150.statcan.gc.ca/t1/tbl1/en/tv.action?pid=381003401

4   John Mullinder, "Suzuki Dead Wrong on Paper's Circular Economy," johnmullinder.ca, October 1, 2020, https://johnmullinder.ca/suzuki-dead-wrong-on-papers-circular-economy/.

5 World Resources Institute, "New Analysis Finds Over 100 Million Hectares of Intact Forest Area Degraded Since 2000," wri.org (press release), September 4, 2014, https://www.wri.org/news/release-new-analysis-finds-over-100-million-hectares-intact-forest-area-degraded-2000; and "New Satellite Data Reveals Massive Tree Cover Loss in Russia and Canada," wri.org (press release), April 2, 2015, http://www.wri.org.news/2015/04/release-new-satellite-data-reveal-massive-tree-cover-loss-russia-and-canada

6 "Canada Largest Contributor to Deforestation Worldwide: Study," *The Huffington Post Canada* online, September 5, 2014, www.huffington-post.ca/2014/09/05/canada-deforestation-worst-in-world_n_5773142.html; "Deforestation Worse than Brazil," (CBC September 5, 2014); "Canada Surpasses Brazil as Global Leader in Deforestation," fernie.com, October 13, 2014, https://fernie.com/blog.canada-surpasses-brazil-as-global-leader-in-deforestation/ Stephen Leahy, "Canada Now World's Leading "Deforestation Nation,'" rabble.ca, October 1, 2014, www.rabble.ca/columnists/2014/10/canada-now-worlds-leading-deforestation-nation.

7 Peter Potapov *et al.* "The Last Frontiers of Wilderness: Tracking: Loss of Intact Forest Landscapes from 2000 to 2013," *Science Advances 3*, no. 1 January, 2017 http://advances.sciencemag.org/content/3/1/e1600821.full.

8 M.C. Hansen *et al.*, "High Resolution Global Maps of 21st-Century Forest Cover Change," *Science 342*, no. 6160, November 15, 2013 www.science.sciencemag.org/content/342/6160/850.

9 Asked recently to back up claims that packaging was a cause of deforestation, the Forest Stewardship Council of Canada instead offered an article that talked about forest cover loss in various countries (See John Mullinder, "FSC Is Misleading Canadians, Say Its Key Packaging Customers," PPEC, April 21, 2020

FOREST

1 FAO and UNEP, *The State of the World's Forests 2020: Forests, Biodiversity and People*, 2020, p. xvii, https://www.fao.org/3/ca8642en/ca8642en.pdf

2 Ibid., and *Global Forest Resources Assessment 2020: Key Findings*, 2020, p.5. https://www.fao.org/3/CA8753EN/CA8753EN.pdf

3 FAO, *Global Forest Resources Assessment 2020: Report Canada* 2020, https://www.fao.org/3/ca9983en/ca9983en.pdf; and FAO, *Global Forests Resources Assessment 2020: Report United States of America*, 2020, https://www.fao.org/3/cb0086en/cb0086en.pdf

4 *Global Forest Resources Assessment 2020: Report Canada* ibid. The FAO also points out the challenges of monitoring and reporting on primary forests in a section of *The State of the World's Forests 2020*, ibid., p.17. "Because of the lack of an operational definition and consistent, easy-to-map indicators, some inconsistencies and bias are inherent in current country-level reporting for FRA 2020 (Bernier *et al*, 2017). Most countries use proxies based on land use and/or land cover to extrapolate data on primary forest and these proxies vary." Because of these concerns, FAO has initiated work to improve reporting on primary forest area and its changes.

5   Natural Resources Canada, *"The State of Canada's Forests Annual Report 2020,"* 2020. https://www.nrcan.gc.ca/our-natural-resources/forests-forestry/state-canadas-forests-report/16496 and Sonja N. Oswalt *et al.*, "Highlights," *Forest Resources of the United States, 2017: A Technical Document Supporting the Forest Service 2020 RPA Assessment*, (Gen. Tech. Report WO-97) US Department of Agriculture Forest Service, March 2019, p. viii. https://www.fs.fed.us/research/publications/gtr/gtr_wo97.pdf

6   FAO, *Global Forest Resources Assessment 2020: Terms and Definitions*, 2020, (working paper 188), 2018, pp. 5-6, https://www.fao.org/3/I8661EN/i8661en.pdf.

FOREST COVER

1   FAO, *Global Forest Resources Assessment 2020, Key Findings*, p. xiii, www.fao.org/3/ca9825en/ca9825en.pdf More than half (54%) of the world's forests is in five countries: the Russian Federation (815 million hectares), Brazil (497 million hectares), Canada (347 million hectares), United States of America (310 million hectares) and China (220 million hectares).

2   The area of Libya is 176 million hectares (Wikipedia, en.wikipedia.org/wiki/Libya). For US comparison, Alaska is 171 million hectares in area (en.wikipedia.org/wiki/Alaska) and for Canadian comparison, Ontario and Manitoba combined make 172 million hectares (en.wikipedia.org/wiki/Ontario and en.wikipedia.org/wiki/Manitoba).

3   *Global Forest Resources Assessment 2020*, ibid., *Key Findings*, p. xi. Between 1990 and 2000, the net change in the annual rate of forest area change was -7.84 million hectares/year. Between 2000 and 2010 this had reduced to -5.17 million hectares/year and between 2010 and 2020 it had further improved to -4.74 million hectares/year.

4   FAO and UNEP, *The State of the World's Forests, 2020, Forests, Biodiversity and People*, 2020, p.9, www.fao.org/documents/card/en/c/ca8642en/

5   *Global Forest Resources Assessment 2020* ibid., p. xi.

6   Natural Resources Canada, *The State of Canada's Forests Annual Report* 2020, p.63. From 348.3 million hectares in 1990 down to 346.9 million hectares in 2018. Partly this is because much of Canada's forest is in remote areas. But it's also because the forests burned by fires, defoliated by insects, or harvested by humans, are regenerated in Canada. The loss is temporary. Another reason for forest stability is Canada's early adoption of the principles and practices of what is called sustainable forest management (SFM). SFM ensures that the renewable resource is managed sustainably for generations to come. In fact, Canada leads the world (the US is ranked third) in the amount of forest independently certified as sustainably managed. It is currently home to 35% (164 million hectares) of the world's certified forests, way ahead of all other countries (Certification Canada "Canadian Statistics:2020 Year-end Statistics," February 2021 http://www.certificationcanada.org/en/statistics/canadian-statistics/ As long as sustainable forest management is practised in this country, Canada will never run out of trees.

7   *Global Forest Resource Assessment 2020*, ibid. US forest cover was estimated to have increased by 7,345,000 hectares (18,149,890 acres) between 1990 and 2020.

8   Author communication with Kathie Rowzie, Two Sides North America. www.two-sidesna.org 18.1 million acres divided by 30 years (604,996 acres/year) divided by 365 days (1657 acres/day) divided by 1.32 acres/NFL football field (1256 football fields).

9   FAO, *The Global Forest Resources Assessment 2020: Terms and Definitions* (working paper 188), 2018, https://www.fao.org/3/I8661EN/i8661en.pdf.

10 The *Global Forest Resources Assessment 2020* definition differs from that of the UN Framework Convention on Climate Change (which covers permanent anthropogenic change only). The UNFCCC also uses a 25% minimum threshold, not the 10% cited here.

FRESH TREES ARE NEEDED BECAUSE PAPER IS IN LANDFILL

1   John Mullinder, "Some Really Deep Thoughts on the Meaning of Life, and Paper," PPEC, March 7, 2014 (Reprinted 2018 in Packaging and the Environment, https://john-mullinder.ca/wp-content/uploads/2018/12/Book-of-Blogs_ July 27-2.pdf., https://john-mullinder.ca/some-really-deep-thoughts-on-the-meaning-of-life-and-paper/).

2   World Business Council for Sustainable Development, *Facts & Trends: Fresh & Recycled Fiber Complementarity*, April 12, 2015, https://www.wbcsd.org/Sector-Projects/Forest-Solutions-Group/Resources/Facts-Trends-Fresh-Recycled-Fiber-Complementarity.

3   "Most Canadian Packaging Board Now 100% Recycled Content," (press release), Paper & Paperboard Packaging Environmental Council (PPEC), September 12, 2019, https://ppec-paper.com/most-canadian-packaging-board-now-100-recycled-content/.

4   For example, the average recycled content of Canadian domestic shipments of containerboard used to make corrugated boxes was 87% in 2020 ("PPEC Releases 2020 Industry Environmental Sustainability Survey Results."(Recycled Content Survey press release), PPEC, July 29, 2021, https://ppec-paper.com/wp-content/uploads/2021/07/PPEC-Press-Release-2020-Recycled-Content-Survey.pdf.

5   It is generally considered that paper fibres can be recycled between four and seven times before the fibres become too short and thin to be of further use in the papermaking process, although a recent laboratory study undertaken by a European university indicated paper fibres could be recycled up to 25 times.

GENERATION (OF WASTE)

1   Waste generation, or the waste stream, is calculated by combining what's diverted with what's sent for disposal. In the example above, 156,000 tonnes of corrugated boxes were diverted and 14,000 tonnes disposed, giving a total generation of 170,000 tonnes. If you want to calculate a *diversion* rate from these numbers you take the diverted tonnes (156,000), divide them by the generated tonnes (170,000), and then multiply the result by 100. The diversion rate in this instance would therefore be 91.76% (92%).

HUNDRED (100%) FULLY, COMPLETELY

1   US Federal Trade Commission, "260.12 Recyclable Claims," *Green Guides (Revised)*, October 1, 2012, https://www.ftc.gov/sites/default/files/attachments/press-releases/ftc-issues-revised-green-guides/greenguides.pdf.

2   Competition Bureau of Canada, "10.1.3 Claims of 'Where Facilities Exist,'" *Environmental Claims: A Guide for Industry and Advertisers*, June 2008, https://www.competition-bureau.gc.ca/eic/site/cb-bc.nsf/vwapi/guide-for-industry-and-advertisers-en.pdf/SFILE/guide-for-industry-and-advertisers-en.pdf.

3   John Mullinder, "What Does '100% Reusable, Recyclable, or, Where Viable Alternatives Do Not Exist, Recoverable' Actually Mean?," PPEC, July 23, 2019 Reposted July 27, 2021 at https://johnmullinder.ca/what-does-100-reusable-recyclable-or-where-viable-alternatives-do-not-exist-recoverable-actually-mean/..

4   Canadian Council of Ministers for the Environment (CCME), *Canada-Wide Action Plan on Zero Plastic Waste, Phase 1*, (PN 1589) June 27, 2019, p.3. https://ccme.ca.en/res/1589_ccmecanada-wideactionplanonzeroplasticwaste_en-secured.pdf.

5   Canadian Council of Ministers for the Environment (CCME), *Strategy for Zero Plastics Waste*, (PN 1583), November 23, 2018, p.5, footnote 2, https://ccme.ca/en/res/strategyonzeroplasticwaste.pdf "Recovery includes all activities at end of life that recover value from plastics waste, rather than disposing of them in landfills or through incineration without energy recovery" Recovery activities are prioritized from high to low value and desirability in accordance with the waste management hierarchy: re-use, mechanical recycling, composting, chemical recycling, and energy recovery.

HYPOCRISY?

1   Laurie David and Heather Reisman, "Modern Paper Use is Wildly Unsustainable. Here's What You Can Do About It," (excerpt adapted from *Imagine It! A Handbook for a Happier Planet* (Toronto: Penguin Random House, 2021), *Popular Science* online, April 6, 2021, https://www.popsci.com/story/environment/what-you-need-to-know-about-paper-a-hidden-environmental-disaster/. See John Mullinder, "Reisman Reveals Woeful Ignorance of Forest and Paper issues," johnmullinder.ca April 18, 2021, https://johnmullinder.ca/reisman-reveals-woeful-ignorance-of-forest-and-paper-issues/.

2   Jennifer Skene (with Shelley Vinyard) *"The Issue with Tissue,"* Natural Resources Defense Council (NRDC) and STAND.earth, February 2019, https://www.stand.earth/sites/default/files/StandEarth-NRDC-IssueWithTissue-Report.pdf. See also **TOILET PAPER.**

3   The NRDC and STAND.earth call the FSC "the world's most creditable independent certifier of responsibly managed forests" and "the only certification system that comes anywhere close to promoting sustainable practices." (*The Issue with Tissue*, ibid.p.17).

4   Todd Paglia, executive director of ForestEthics, quoted in "FPAC Commits to New Forest Management Approach to Mimic Elements of Nature," (press release by the Forest Products Association of Canada) Fastmarket's RISI Technology Channels (on-

line), January 14, 2016, https://technology.risiinfo.com/mills/north-america/fpac-commits-to-new-forest-management-approach-mimic-elements-nature. Other participating environmental organisations included the Canadian Parks and Wilderness Society, Ivey Foundation, The Nature Conservancy, TNC Canada, International Boreal Conservation Campaign and the Schad Foundation.

5 "Earth Friendly Bagasse Sugarcane Bowls Are Perfect for Hot and Cold Food," ecokloud.com. n.d., www.ecokloud.com/biodegradable/compostable/bagasse-bowls.html; "Paper Soup Bowls with PLA Lining," ecokloud.com, n.d., www.ecokloud.com/biodegradable/compostable/paper-pla-bowls.html; and "Earth Friendly Paper Hot Cups with Corn PLA Lining," ecokloud.com, n.d., www.ecokloud.com/biodegradable/compostable/paper-pla-hot-cups.html, all accessed August 9, 2021.

"KILLING" AND "SAVING" TREES

1 Forests hold more than 75% of the world's terrestrial biodiversity, according to the FAO/UNEP's *State of the World's Forests, 2016: Forests and Agriculture: Land Use Challenges and Opportunities*, 2016, p.2, https://www.fao.org/3/i5588e/i5588e.pdf.

2 According to a Toronto study, having 10 more trees on a city block improved health perception, and made people feel seven years younger! This tree psychology study by Professor Marc Berman is quoted in Amy Fleming, "The Importance of Urban Forests: Why Money Really Does Grow on Trees" (book review of Jill Jonnes, *Urban Forests, A Natural History of Trees and People in the American Cityscape*), *Guardian* online, October 12, 2016, www.the.guardian.com/cities/2016/oct/12/importance-urban-forests-money-grow-trees

3 The following are edited versions of three harvesting techniques described in the National Forestry Database Glossary ("Harvesting and Regeneration," http://nfdp.ccfm.org/en/glossary.php): Clear-cutting (also known as even-aged management where the maximum difference in tree age permitted is usually 10-20 years) is a method of regenerating an even-aged forest stand in which new seedlings become established in fully exposed micro-environments after removal of most or all existing trees. Regeneration can originate naturally or artificially. Clear-cutting can be done in blocks, strips or patches and in stages over several operating seasons. The selection method (uneven-aged management, tree age usually greater than 10-20 years) regenerates a forest stand and maintains an uneven-aged structure by removing some trees in all size classes either singly or in small groups or strips. And thinning is a cutting made in an immature crop or stand primarily to accelerate increment but also by suitable selection to improve the average form of the trees that remain.

4 World Resources Institute and the World Business Council for Sustainable Development, *Sustainable Procurement of Wood and Paper-based Products*, http://sustainableforestproducts.org/Sustainable_Forest_Management

5 A homogenous even-aged forest like Canada's boreal lends itself to clear-cutting. Here the main driver of forest renewal is wildfires (which can be 10 times the size of any clear-cut). Partial and selective cutting make more sense in deciduous uneven-aged forest types found further south in temperate forests where mortality and renewal patterns occur at a much smaller scale, most often at the tree level. The variety of species

that are found in these forests is much higher and they are generally more tolerant to grow under a tree cover. In effect, the nature of the particular forest ecosystem determines how the trees should be "killed."

6   "FPAC Commits to New Forest Management Approach to Mimic Elements of Nature," (press release for Forest Products Association of Canada), Fastmarket's RISI Technology Channels (online), January 14, 2016, https://technology.risiinfo.com/mills/north-america/fpac-commits-new-forest-management-approach-mimic-elements-nature.

7   In Canada, provincial foresters use the growth rate of trees (which vary by species across the country) and their knowledge of tree science to establish what they consider to be a sustainable wood supply for both softwoods (spruce, pine, fir) and hardwoods (aspen and poplar). In each case, the amount harvested is currently way below what the provinces estimate is sustainable. (National Forestry Database: Wood Supply nfdp.ccfm.org/en/data/woodsupply.php, accessed August 1, 2021). With more burned and insect-infected forests today, foresters are finding that the health of the forest (to what extent it can be salvaged) is of increasing importance in the selection process.

8   Natural Resources Canada, *The State of Canada's Forests, Annual Report 2020*, p.17, https://www.nrcan.gc.ca/our-natural-resources/forests-forestry/state-canadas-forests-report/16496. Some 77% is on provincial Crown land, 13% on territorial Crown land, almost 2% on federal Crown land with the remaining forest area privately owned (just over 6%) and Indigenous-owned (about 2%). Private ownership in the US is 56% according to the US Department of Agriculture.

9   Simply put, sustainable forest management (SFM) is a way of looking at a forest for all its values: social, economic, environmental, and cultural. It's an approach that considers not just wood harvested and local employment, but also streams protected and wildlife habitat conserved (Canadian Council of Forest Ministers, *Measuring our Progress: Putting Sustainable Forest Management into Practice Across Canada and Beyond*, 2020, https://www.ccfm.org/wp-content/uploads/2020/08/Measuring-our-progress-Putting-sustainable-forest-management-into-practice-across-Canada-and-beyond.pdf.

10   The following countries of the Montreal Process (https://www.fs.fed.us/research/sustain/montreal-process.php) represent 90% of the world's temperate and boreal forests, 49% of all forests, 58% of planted forests, 49% of global roundwood production, and 31% of the world's population (Argentina, Australia, Canada, Chile, China, Japan, Republic of Korea, Mexico, New Zealand, Russian Federation, United States of America and Uruguay). The Montreal Process has seven criteria and 54 indicators www.montrealprocess.org

11   Today, for example, Natural Resources Canada uses some 54 sustainability indicators to track the country's progress. The indicators are wide-ranging: from biological diversity to eco-system productive capacity, health, and vitality; from the conservation of soil and water resources to the maintenance of the forest's contribution to global carbon cycles; and from the maintenance and enhancement of long-term multiple socio-economic benefits to a legal, institutional and economic framework for forest conservation and sustainable management. Canadian Council of Forest Ministers, *Criteria and Indicators,* www.cfs.nrcan.gc.ca/pubwarehouse/pfs/32560.pdf

12 *Certification Canada* certificationcanada.org/en/home/ Canada has 35% of the world's certified forest, the Russian Federation 11%, the United States 9%, Australia 6% and Sweden 5%. Just 11% of the world's forests are independently certified.

13 Dovetail Partners, "Contrary to Popular Thinking, Going Paperless Does Not Save Trees," (white paper produced on behalf of Two Sides North America), February 8, 2016, http://www.twosidesna.org/download/Dovetail-Report-February-2016.pdf

14 What does cement have to do with forestry? The Cement Association of Canada recently co-funded an environmental group's highly critical study of Ontario logging practices. The association is lobbying against the greater use of engineered wood, a substitute for more emissions-intensive cement products in the building sector.

15 A plastic lobby group's favourite slogan while campaigning against a possible plastic bag ban in Montreal recently was "Save a Tree."

16 See **SUGARCANE (BAGASSE)**.

17 See **ENVIRONMENTALLY FRIENDLY, ECO-FRIENDLY.**

18 See **SUGARCANE (BAGASSE)** and the wheat straw example in **"TREE-FREE."**

19 There are numerous examples of lower consumption of paper materials through light-weighting and right-sizing (smaller and lighter sheets, eliminating or reducing layers, reconfiguring box flaps, removing air space between the product and its packaging). One celebrated project by the Paper & Paperboard Packaging Environmental Council (PPEC) reduced fibre consumption by an estimated 100,000 tonnes a year by amending the shipping rules on corrugated containers. See "Reduction: Making Do With Less" PPEC Factsheet 24-2019, www.ppec-paper.com/pdfFiles/factsheets/2019/The3Rs/FS24-2019.pdf

20 While it is *technically* accurate that a 100% recycled mill does not "kill" any trees itself, it would not have any paper fibre to make products with unless someone else in the paper life cycle had "killed" a tree first. The paper life cycle requires an infusion of fresh virgin fibre as recycled fibres become progressively weaker. See John Mullinder, "Some Really Deep Thoughts on the Meaning of Life, and Paper," PPEC, March 7, 2014. www.ppec-paper.com/some-really-deep-thoughts/

"OLD-GROWTH" FOREST

1 See **FOREST** for an outline of how the United Nations Food and Agriculture Organization (FAO) classifies the world's forests as naturally regenerating and planted, with sub-categories including primary forest. See also the discussion in **"ANCIENT" FORESTS.**

2 FAO, *Global Forest Resources Assessment 2020, Report, Canada.* www.fao.org/forest-resources-assessment/fra-2020/country-reports/en/

3 Natural Resources Canada, *The State of Canada's Forests, Annual Report, 2020,* 2020. More than 90% of Canada's forests are found on publicly-owned land including 77% on provincial Crown land, 13% on territorial Crown land and almost 2% on federal Crown land. The remaining forest is privately owned (just over 6%) and Indigenous owned (about 2%).

4   Forest Products Association of Canada, *Calculating the Extent of Conservation Lands within Canada's Managed Forests*, 2020. Protected forest land cover of 35.46 million hectares (10.5%)

5   Natural Resources Canada http://www.nrcan.gc.ca/our-natural-resources/forests/sustainable-forest-management/conservation-and-protection-canadas-forests/17501

6   *Calculating the Extent of Conservation Lands within Canada's Managed Forests,* ibid.

7   Ibid.

8   Ibid.

9   Ibid.

10 Forests Products Association of Canada, *Old Growth Forests, Natural Diversity Across Canada.*

11 National Forest Inventory (Canada) database, *Table 14.1. Area (1000 ha) of forest land by species group, age class and terrestrial ecozone in Canada. https://nfi.nfis.org/resources/general/summaries/to/en/NFI/html/NFI_T14_LSAGE20_AREA_en.html* The 201+ category totals 14.9 million hectares of 347.6 million hectares of forest land (4.3%). Most (64%) Canadian trees are under 100 years old (222.5 million hectares of 347.6 million hectares). Only 1% of the Canadian boreal forest is 201+ years old. The boreal forest is considered to include parts of the Taiga Plains, Taiga Shield, Boreal Shield, Boreal Plains, Taiga Cordillera, Boreal Cordillera and the Hudson Plains totalling 270 million hectares of forest. Some 3.1 million hectares of this is 201+ years old (1%).   https://nfi.nfis.org/resources/general/summaries/to/en/BORE_T14_LSAGE20_AREA_en.html

12 National Forest Inventory (Canada) database, *Table 14.1* ibid. The Montane Cordillera contains 6.2 million hectares of 201+ plus forest and the Pacific Maritime ecozone 6.0 million hectares (together 81.75% of the total for this category of 14.9 million hectares). The most numerous species in this category in these two ecozones are fir, hemlock, and spruce (the same pattern as for Canada as a whole).

13 "Old Growth Forests," Government of British Columbia, last updated June 24, 2021. *www.gov.bc.ca/gov/content/industry/forestry/managing-our-forest-resources/old-growth-forests#Defining* See also *Old Growth Policy for Ontario's Crown Forests,* Government of Ontario, 2003, https://docs.ontario.ca/documents/2830/policy-old-growth-eng-aoda.pdf. Gouvernement du Québec, Ministère des Forêts, de la Faune et des Parcs, Intégration des enjeux écologiques dans les plans d'aménagement forestier intégré de 2018-2023, Mai 2015, https://mffp.gouv.qc.ca/wp-content/uploads/Cahier_3_3_erabliere.pdf.

OMISSIONS

1   See John Mullinder, "False Claims and Sloppy Journalism Add to the Public Confusion About Deforestation in Canada, " johnmullinder.ca, January 13, 2020, https://johnmullinder.ca/false-claims-and-sloppy-journalism-add-to-the-public-confusion-about-deforestation-in-Canada/ in response to Ivan Semeniuk, "'Logging Scars' Show that Impact of Deforestation is Underestimated, Analysis Reveals" *Globe and Mail,* December

3, 2019, updated April 4, 2020, https://www.theglobeandmail.com/canada/article-logging-scars-show-impact-of-deforestation-in-canada-is-worse-than/.

2   Extrapolating estimates from 27 study sites in one region to the total harvest area of Ontario is problematic. Most of these study sites were harvested using "full-tree" harvesting some 20 or even 30 years ago. And it is uncertain to what extent those logging methods are still applied today. Not all harvested areas in Ontario are forests that have never been harvested before, either. The forest losses claimed in the study, then, should not be extrapolated to the whole of Ontario, and especially not to those areas that already have an existing road network.

3   The major causes of deforestation in Canada at the time of the article were conversion of forest land to agriculture (33%); oil and gas exploration (24%); hydro-electric development (12%); mining (9%); urban development (9%); transportation (5%); forestry (4%); industry (3%); and recreation (1%), according to Natural Resources Canada, *The State of Canada's Forests Annual Report, 2018*, https://www.cfs.nrcan.gc.ca/pubwarehouse/pdfs/39336.pdf. Ontario and Canada follow UN guidelines on measuring deforestation and this includes not counting small (meaning less than one hectare in size) "change events" such as landing areas or small plots of agricultural land that have recently been reforested. See **DEFORESTATION**.

4   The three people interviewed in the article were the Wildlands League author of the study; someone from the New York-based Natural Resources Defense Council which helped fund the study; and a professor with the University of Toronto Forestry Team who according to the study (p. 167) provided "thoughtful guidance."

5   The Cement Association of Canada paid some of the field expenses for the study (p. 167). What's cement got to do with forestry issues? It just happens that the Cement Association was lobbying against the greater use of engineered wood, a substitute for more emissions-intensive cement products in the building sector at the time.

6   National Deforestation Monitoring System (NDMS), Natural Resources Canada and the Canadian Forest Service.

7   Valerie Langer, "What's in the Box? Part 1," Canopy, November 6, 2019, https://www.canopyplanet.org/whats-in-the-box-part-/

8   "Most Canadian Packaging Board Now 100% Recycled Content," (press release), Paper & Paperboard Packaging Environmental Council (PPEC), September 12, 2019, https://www.ppec-paper.com/most-canadian-packaging-board-now-100-recycled-content/

9   Paper & Paperboard Packaging Environmental Council (PPEC), "Pioneering the Recycling of Old Boxboard Cartons," (Factsheet 31-2019), PPEC, 2019, https://www.ppec-paper.com/pdfFiles/factsheets/2019/The3Rs/FS31-2019.pdf.

10   John Mullinder, "Canopy Makes More Embarrassing 'Boo-Boos,'" PPEC, March 2, 2020, Reposted March 17, 2020, https://johnmullinder.ca/canopy-makes-more-embarrassing-boo-boos/

11   Natural Resources Canada, *The State of Canada's Forests, Annual Report, 2020*, 2020, https://www.nrcan.gc.ca/our-natural-resources/forests-forestry/state-canadas-forests-report/16496.

12 The results of the January 2018 survey appear in John Mullinder, *Deforestation in Canada and Other Fake News* (Victoria, BC: Tellwell Talent, 2018). The 17 environmental groups surveyed were the Canadian Environmental Law Association, Canadian Parks and Wilderness Society, Canadian Wildlife League, Canopy, Earth Day, Earthroots, Ecojustice, Ecology Action, Environmental Defence Canada, Forest Stewardship Council of Canada, Global Forest Watch Canada, Greenpeace Canada, Nature Conservancy of Canada, Sierra Club (BC), Stand (formerly ForestEthics), David Suzuki Foundation, and World Wildlife Fund Canada.

13 Natural Resources Canada, *The State of Canada's Forests, Annual Report 2020*, 2020, https://www.nrcan.gc.ca/our-natural-resources/forests-forestry/state-canadas-forests-report/16496.

PACKAGING WASTE

1 There is a useful graph showing utilization, overpackaging and under-packaging in ISO 18602:2013. ISO, *Packaging and the Environment: Optimization of the Packaging System*, January 15, 2013, p. vii, https://www.sis.se/api/document/preview/915736/.

2 On average, packaging accounts for about 5% of the energy used in the life cycle of a food product, according to the Climate Collaborative (https://www.climatecollaborative.com/packaging).

3 Canadian Council of Ministers of the Environment, *National Packaging Protocol 2000 Final Report*, (PN 1511), June 22,2000, p. 27, https://ccme.ca/en/res/nationalpackagingprotocolfinalreport_e.pdf. This Statistics Canada monitoring exercise over 10 years and its final results covered 31 separate industry sectors of the economy and 32 different packaging material types, using surveys as well as information derived from Statistics Canada's international trade merchandise data and a national study of residential recycling. Some 10,000 surveys representing a total survey frame of almost 400,000 businesses were sent out with the 61% response rate regarded by Statistics Canada as consistent with other similar surveys. Two significant findings of the survey were that over 70% of all packaging consumed in Canada was reused or recycled, and that industrial recycling (mainly of old corrugated boxes) accounted for almost 75% of all packaging recycling (Tables 1 and 29). While this survey is now obviously dated, it still remains the most comprehensive survey on packaging that Canada has. Of course, packaging has been continuously light-weighted over the years, and there is more (lighter) plastic packaging today and less (heavier) glass.

4 Statistics Canada, *Waste Management Industry Survey Business and Government Sectors 1996*, Table 2.2 *Non-Hazardous Materials by Source and by Province and Territory, 1996*, shows Canada's total solid waste of 20.6 million tonnes. The National Packaging Survey for the same year (see endnote 3) gave a packaging disposal number of 2.64 million tonnes (so 12.8% of the total). If sewage and sewage sludge, hazardous waste, and construction and demolition waste are removed from the equation, this reduces the disposal pie to 13.3 million tonnes (increasing packaging's "share" to 19.8%).

5 While most packaging is used by the industrial, commercial and institutional (IC & I) sectors of the economy, current indications are that packaging represents only

about 10% of residential disposal tonnages. Households in the province of Ontario, for example, sent 3.9 million tonnes of waste for disposal in 2018 (Statistics Canada), some 405,845 tonnes of that (10%) being packaging from the province's Blue Box program (Stewardship Ontario Blue Box disposal data, 2018). Ontario's Resource Productivity and Recovery Authority (RPRA) however, has household disposal at a much lower number (2.4 million tonnes) which boosts packaging's share to 16.9%.

6 US Environmental Protection Agency (EPA): *Advancing Sustainable Materials Management 2018 Fact Sheet, Table 4, Generation, Recycling, Composting, Other Food Management Pathways, Combustion with Energy Recovery and Landfilling of Products in MSW, 2018*, December 2018, p.12, https://www.epa.gov/sites/default/files/2021-01/documents/2018_ff_fact_sheet_dec_2020_fnl_508.pdf. Unlike Canada, the US EPA measures "municipal solid waste," which it defines as not including industrial, hazardous or construction and demolition waste (p.5). In Table 4, the Total Containers and Packaging category was held responsible for 30.47 million short tons of disposal (21% of MSW).

"PAPERLESS"

1 Section 8.3: "If a self-declared environmental claim involves a comparison with other products, then a description of the method used, the results of any tests of those products, or any of the assumptions made shall be clearly stated." Section 9: "Comparative claims always require an explanatory statement to identify the benchmark against which they have been evaluated. The comparison shall only be made using a published standard or recognized test method." Competition Bureau Canada, "8.3 Access to Information" and "9 Comparative Claims," *Environmental Claims: A Guide for Industry and Advertisers*, June 2008, https://www.competitionbureau.gc.ca/eic/site/cb-bc.nsf/eng/04607.html US Federal Trade Commission, "260.2 Interpretation and Substantiation of Environmental Marketing Claims," *Green Guides (Revised)*, October 1, 2012, https://www.ftc.gov/sites/default/files/attachments/press-releases/ftc-issues-revised-green-guides/greenguides.pdf.

2 Paper industry trade group Two Sides North America points out that paper comes from a renewable resource, is made using mostly renewable carbon-neutral biomass energy, and is recyclable and widely recycled. See "Electronic Communication has Environmental Impacts" (Myths & Facts), twosidesna.org, n.d., https://twosidesna.org/e-media-also-has-environmental-impacts/; "Paper or Digital? Consumer Choice is Being Removed by Corporations" (fact sheet), twosidesna.org, July 7, 2017, https://twosidesna.org/US/paper-or-digital-consumer-choice-is-being-removed-by-corporations/; "Electronic Communication," (fact sheet), twosidesna.org, January 2021, https://twosidesna.org/wp-content/uploads/sites/16/2021/06/Electronic-Communication-REV-0621.pdf; and "Paperless 'Green' Claims" (fact sheet), twosides.na.org, January 2021, https://twosidesna.org/wp-content/uploads/sites/16/2021/03/Paperless-Green-Claims-2021-FINAL2.pdf.

3 Cisco estimates that by 2023 North America will have 345 million internet users (up from 328 million in 2018) and 5 billion networked devices/connections, up from 3 billion in 2018 (*Cisco Internet Annual Report, 2020*). All this requires energy. According to a US Department of Energy report on *Data Center Usage* (2016), data centers in the United States consumed an estimated 70 billion kWh, representing about 1.8% of total US elec-

tricity consumption. Based on current trend estimates, US data centers are projected to consume approximately 73 billion kWh in 2020. This energy consumption does not include the energy required to build, power, or recharge the devices. An analysis by the *National Renewable Energy Laboratory* (2015) of 113 Information Communications Technology (ICT) companies in the United States showed that 14% of the energy consumed was from renewable energy. This compares to 65% of energy demand met at US pulp and paper mills by carbon-neutral biomass and renewable fuels in 2018 (*American Forest and Paper Association 2020 Sustainability Report*).

4   The manufacture of a computer, in addition to fossil fuels, chemicals and water requires the extraction of precious metals (gold and platinum) and rare earth minerals used in cell phone batteries and liquid crystal display screens, as well as hazardous materials like lead, bromine, arsenic, chlorine, mercury and cadmium (Statista, 2020 and Organisme Agence de l'environnement et de la maîtrise de l'énergie, France, 2017) quoted in "Electronic Communication Has Environmental Impacts" (Myths & Facts), twosidesna.org, n.d., https://twosidesna.org/wp-content/uploads/sites/16/2018/05/E-Media-also-has-environmental-impacts.pdf.

5   *Global E-waste Monitor* (2020) reports that the United States and Canada collectively generated 7.7 million tonnes of electronic waste in 2019 (small electronic equipment, screens and monitors, and telecommunications equipment) with only 15% of it sent on for recycling. Most e-waste was either dumped or burned rather than being collected for recycling or reuse. Recent research cited by *Global E-waste Monitor* indicates unregulated e-waste is associated with increasing numbers of adverse health effects (altered neuro-development and learning, DNA damage, cardiovascular and respiratory problems, skin diseases, hearing loss and cancer).

6   *Busting the Myths: A Study of US and Canadian Consumer Perceptions and Attitudes Towards Print and Paper,* Two Sides and Toluna, 2019, United States: Canada: https://twosidesna.org/wp-content/uploads/sites/16/2019/06/TSNA_BustingTheMythsReport_USA_Online.pdf;

7   A study by a Danish company, Natur-Energi, found that sending invoices by email actually *increased* their overall costs. That's because 59% of customers had to be sent a reminder, while only 29% of customers receiving the invoice via mail required a follow-up message (Fresh Data, 2013), quoted in *Paper or Digital?* ibid.

8   *Busting the Myths*, ibid.

PIZZA BOXES

1   *Incorporation of Post-Consumer Pizza Boxes in the Recovered Fiber Stream, Impact of Grease and Cheese on Finished Product Quality* (study), WestRock 2020. https://www.westrock.com/greasecheesestudy

2   Haley study, February 2015, and John Mullinder "Retailers Can't Duck Food Safety Issues When Pushing Growers to Reuse Crates," PPEC, March 28, 2017 at https://ppec-paper.com/retailers-cant-duck-food-safety-issues-pushing-growers-re-use-crates/.

PRISTINE AND UNDISTURBED FOREST

1   Natural Resources Canada, *The State of Canada's Forests, Annual Report 2020*, 2020. https://www.nrcan.gc.ca/our-natural-resources/forests-forestry/state-canadas-forests-report/16496. Some 16.39 million hectares of Canadian forest was defoliated by insects and beetles in 2018 and 1.84 million hectares burned by forest fires in 2019. The harvested area, principally for lumber, was 0.74 million hectares, which by law must be successfully regenerated after harvest.

"RECOVERABLE"

1   Plastics recovery apparently means everything other than dumping plastics in landfill or burning it without energy recovery. According to the CCME's *Strategy for Zero Plastics Waste*, "Recovery includes all activities at end of life that recover value from plastics waste, rather than disposing of them in landfill or through incineration without energy recovery." Recovery activities are prioritized from high to low value and desirability in accordance with the waste management hierarchy" reuse, mechanical recycling, composting, chemical recycling, and energy recovery. Canadian Council of Ministers for the Environment (CCME), *Strategy for Zero Plastics Waste* (PN 1583), November 23, 2018, p.5, footnote 2, https://ccme.ca/en/res/strategyonzeroplasticwaste.pdf.

RECOVERY AND RECYCLING RATES

1   John Mullinder, "What Does '100% Reusable, Recyclable, or, Where Viable Alternatives Do Not Exist, Recoverable' Actually Mean?," PPEC, July 23, 2019 (Reposted July 27, 2021, https://johnmullinder.ca/what-does-100-reusable-recyclable-or-where-viable-alternatives-do-not-exist-recoverable-actually-mean/. See also Canadian Council of Ministers for the Environment (CCME), *Strategy for Zero Plastics Waste*, (PN 1583), November 23, 2018, p.5, footnote 2, https://ccme.ca/en/res/strategyonzeroplasticwaste.pdf.

2   There is a good discussion of these issues in *Definitions for the Circular Economy in Canada* by Dan Lantz of Crow's Nest Environmental, October 2019 (available through the Paper & Paperboard Packaging Environmental Council (PPEC) www.ppec-paper.com). Under European Union (EU) Regulations, recently updated targets for diversion include only reuse and recycling (55% by 2025, 60% by 2030, and 65% by 2035). Under the Circular Economy Action Plan (March 4, 2019), the packaging target relates only to the percentage that is recycled (65% by 2025 and 75% by 2030).

3   John Mullinder, "The Inconvenient Truth About Packaging Waste in Canada," PPEC, July 22, 2010 (Reprinted 2018 in *Packaging and the Environment*, https://johnmullinder.ca/wp-content/uploads/2018/12/Book-of-Blogs July 27-2.pdf).In 1997, the average packaging recycling rate for the 15 countries of the European Commission (EU 15) was 46%. Canada's recycling rate from a year earlier (Statistics Canada for the Canadian Council of Ministers for the Environment, 1996 National Packaging Monitoring Survey results, *Table 1*, was basically the same (45%).

4   Or maybe they should be called Material Capture Facilities because what happens to the materials (recycling or recovery) doesn't occur until the material goes to the next step?

5   CSSA (Canadian Stewardship Services Alliance) *2020 Annual Steward Meeting: Report to Stewards*, October 21, 2020. The document makes clear it is talking about recycling systems and recycling performance but then uses the words *recovery rates and targets* in the sections on Recycle BC, Multi-Material Stewardship Western, and Multi-Material Stewardship Manitoba. The section on Stewardship Ontario is the only one to use the words recycling rate. In its separate data reports, however, Stewardship Ontario uses the term *recovery rate*.

6   British Columbia does have a separate sub-category for recovery within its program for materials captured and sent for alternative fuel substitution.

7   According to the bill's sponsor, "We do not want these chemical approaches … to poison the environment or the populations that live near these facilities." "We just say that you can't call it recycling, and require that whatever facilities the chemical association wants to do, that they be included in the comprehensive study by EPA and the National Academy of Sciences, so we can understand their cumulative impacts on human health and the environment, so we can adequately update our clean air and clean water regulations." Colin Staub, "Chemical Recycling Now at the Center of National Plastics Debate," *Plastics Recycling Update,* March 31, 2021, https://resource-recycling.com/plastics/2021/03/31/chemical-recycling-now-at-the-center-of-national-plastics-debate/.

8   *"Definitions within the Circular Economy in Canada,"* ibid. Australia makes a distinction between closed-loop recycling (glass bottles back into glass bottles) and open-loop recycling (glass bottles into fibreglass), but glass used as roadbed materials or as an aggregate is not considered to be recycling. The United Kingdom accepts glass crushed for blasting as recycling but back-filling operations (when a suitable waste replaces a non-waste in landscape engineering) is not considered recycling.

9   Mary Ann Remolador, *Northeast MRF Glass Survey Report*, Northeast Recycling Council (NERC), October 2018, https://portal-test.ct.gov/-/media/DEEP/waste_management_and_disposal/Solid_Waste_Management_Plan/October2018/NERCPresentation-MWMAOct7pdf.pdf?rev=5bb3c52c028b4b6998b5e6ee98cd1b2d&hash=94F30C343EAE-CF39E0FD7C4B9AEED934.

10   The US EPA bases its generation numbers on a combination of data from industry and trade associations, state and federal government sources, and waste sample studies. It makes adjustments for imports and exports and product life times. The recycling rate is measured at the point a material leaves the material recovery facility for an end-market. In Canada, the Blue Box stewardship programs rely on brand owner and retailer reports on the materials they have placed in the residential marketplace, on municipal data on what's in garbage and recycling, and on representative waste composition audits that are statistically extrapolated to the rest of the province. As noted, they vary in whereabouts they measure to determine a recycling rate.

11   Yield losses at paper recycling mills can be as high as 35% and at plastics facilities 50%. Together these materials represent a significant portion of materials sent for recycling so 25% is assumed to be a reasonable average yield loss for Blue Box materials as a whole.

12   Recent regulations for Ontario's Blue Box program confirm that the Ministry of Environment, Conservation and Parks favours the higher recycling targets approach.

See John Mullinder, "Ontario Blue Box Will Struggle to Make 60% Diversion and None of the Ministry's Proposed New Targets Will Be Reached," PPEC, December 16, 2020, before the regulations were introduced (Reposted date December 27, 2021 https://johnmullinder.ca/ontario-blue-box-will-struggle-to-make-60-diversion-and-none-of-the-ministrys-proposed-new-targets-will-be-reached/.   The earlier proposed targets for some materials have been reduced in the subsequent regulation but the ministry clearly hopes (while not spelling it out) for an overall Blue Box diversion rate of 75% to 80%.

RECYCLABLE

1 The US and Canadian guidelines are based on ISO 14021, *Environmental Labels and Declarations- Self-Declared Environmental Claims (Type 11 Environmental Labelling)*. https://www.iso.org/standard/66652.html

2 Competition Bureau Canada, "4.3 Specifics of CAN/CSA-ISO 14021 (Clause 5.7d),"*Environmental Claims: A Guide for Industry and Advertisers,* June 2008, https://www.competitionbureau.gc.ca/eic/site/cb-bc.nsf/eng/04607.html The US *Green Guides* give two examples of a service. 260.12(d), Example 8: "A manufacturer of one-time use cameras, with dealers in a substantial majority of communities, operates a take-back program that collects those cameras through all of its dealers. The manufacturer reconditions the cameras for resale and labels them "Recyclable through our dealership network." This claim is not deceptive, even though the cameras are not recyclable through conventional curbside or drop-off recycling programs." 260.12(d) Example 9: "A manufacturer advertising its toner cartridges for computer printers as "Recyclable. Contact your local dealer for details." Although all of the company's dealers recycle cartridges, the dealers are not located in a substantial majority of communities where cartridges are sold. Therefore, the claim is deceptive. The manufacturer should qualify its claim consistent with 260.11(b)(2)." US Federal Trade Commission, "260.12 Recyclable Claims," *Green Guides (Revised),* October 1, 2012, https://www.ftc.gov/news-events/media-resources/truth-advertising/green-guides.

3 "10.1.3. General," *Environmental Claims,* ibid.

4 "260.12(a) Recyclable Claims," *Green Guides (Revised),* ibid.

5 "10.1.3. General," *Environmental Claims,* ibid.

6 "260.12(b)(1) Recyclable Claims," *Green Guides (Revised),* ibid.

7 "10.7.2. Recyclable," *Environmental Claims,* ibid.

8 "260.12(d), Example 4," *Green Guides (Revised),* ibid. The "Sometimes Recyclable" logo of the How2recycle program where it says "Check Locally" and "Not recycled in all communities" is apparently acceptable to the FTC. Between 20% and 59% of US consumers must have access to recycling for a package to use this logo. https://how2recycle.info.

9 "260.12(b)(2) Recyclable Claims," *Green Guides (Revised)* ibid.: "… Marketers may always qualify recyclable claims by stating the percentage of consumers or communities that have access to facilities that recycle the item. Alternatively, marketers may use

qualifications that vary in strength depending on facility availability. The lower the level of access to an appropriate facility is, the more strongly the marketer should emphasize the limited availability of recycling for the product. For example, if recycling facilities are available to slightly less than a substantial majority of consumers or communities where the item is sold, a marketer may qualify a recyclable claim by stating: 'This product (package) may not be recyclable in your area' or "Recycling facilities for this product (package) may not exist in your area.' If recycling facilities are available only to a few customers, marketers should use stronger clarifications. For example, a marketer in this situation may qualify its recyclable claim by stating: 'This product (package) is recyclable only in the few communities that have appropriate recycling facilities.'"

10   An area of further confusion is when some packaging types (for example, plastic stand-up pouches) are recyclable, but other similar pouches are not. Municipalities are reluctant to confuse consumers.

11   "260.12(c) Recyclable Claims," *Green Guides (Revised)*, ibid.: "Marketers can make an unqualified recyclable claim for a product or package if the entire product or package, *excluding minor incidental* (emphasis added) components, is recyclable. For items that are partially made of recyclable components, marketers should clearly and prominently qualify the recyclable claim to avoid deception about which parts are recyclable." "260.12(d) Recyclable Claims" *Green Guides (Revised)*, ibid.: "If any component significantly limits the ability to recycle the item, any recyclable claim would be deceptive." The FTC gives ten examples. Example 1 is where it is not clear whether the claim refers to the product or the package. That needs to be clarified. Example 2 is of a nationally marketed yogurt container prominently displaying the resin identification code close to the product name and logo. Such conspicuous use of the resin code is considered to be a claim for recyclability. If, however, the resin code is embedded on the bottom of the container (that is, in a less conspicuous position) that is not considered to be a recyclable claim. Example 6 is of "a package labelled *"Includes some recyclable material."* The package is composed of four layers of different materials, bonded together. One of the layers is made from recyclable material, but the others are not. While programs for recycling the 25 percent of the package that consists of recyclable material are available to a substantial majority of consumers, only a few of those programs have the capability to separate the recyclable layer from the non-recyclable layers." The FTC says a recyclable claim here is deceptive because it does not specify the portion of the product that is recyclable, and it doesn't disclose the limited availability of facilities that could process multi-layer products or materials.

RECYCLED

1   Sarah Edwards and Sydnee Grushack, "The 50 States of Recycling: A State-by-State Assessment of Containers and Packaging Recycling Rates," Eunomia, March 30, 2021, https://www.eunomia.co.uk/reports-tools/the-50-states-of-recycling-a-state-by-state-assessment-of-containers-and-packaging-recycling-rates/. The Eunomia table recreated in this section shows process losses and yields for different materials. Unfortunately, the totals for two of them (ferrous cans and glass) do not add up to 100%. The Eunomia ferrous can total is 1% shy and the glass category is out by 9%. Eunomia was alerted to this fact but had not

provided any explanation by publication deadline. The Eunomia ferrous can number has been adjusted slightly but Eunomia's glass numbers are not shown.

2 Even though a paper recycling mill may receive (and pay for) 10 tonnes of paper for recycling, it does not claim the 10 tonnes received as recycled content. It only counts the tonnage of the material shipped out the door (say 9 tonnes) as recycled content.

3 John Mullinder, "The End-Markets Get No Love!" PPEC, February 19, 2016 and "The Good, the Bad, and the Ugly About Ontario's Blue Box," PPEC, January 13, 2017, were both reprinted 2018 in *Packaging and the Environment*, https://johnmullinder.ca/wp-content/uploads/2018/12/Book-of-Blogs_July_27-2.pdf.

RECYCLED CONTENT

1 This item is updated from a section in John Mullinder, *Deforestation in Canada and Other Fake News* (Victoria, BC: Tellwwell Talent, 2018), and "False Arguments Being Used to Promote Post-Consumer Recycled Content," PPEC, May 26, 2020, http://www.johnmullinder.ca/false-arguments-being-used-to-promote-post-consumer-recycled-content

2 There are various definitions of "Circular economy." This is Environment and Climate Change Canada's: "The circular economy is a different way of doing business. The way our economies extract, use, then dispose of resources is putting pressure on our natural systems, communities, and health. This is a linear economy – it moves in a straight line from resource extraction to waste disposal. In a circular economy, nothing is waste. The circular economy retains and recovers as much value as possible from resources by reusing, repairing, refurbishing, remanufacturing, repurposing, or recycling products and materials. It's about using valuable resources wisely, thinking about waste as a resource instead of a cost, and finding innovative ways to better the environment and the economy." https://www.canada.ca/en/services/environment/conservation/sustainability/circular-economy.html

RECYCLED VERSUS RECYCLABLE

1 John Mullinder, "Some of the Worst Performing Blue Box Materials Pay the Lowest Fees," PPEC, April 2, 2020 https://johnmullinder.ca/some-of-the-worst-performing-blue-box-materials-pay-the-lowest-fees/.

RECYCLING

1 Definition of sustainable materials management (by the US Environmental Protection Agency): "Sustainable materials management (SMM) is a systemic approach to using and reusing materials more productively over their entire life cycles. It represents a change in how our society thinks about the use of natural resources and environmental protection. By examining how materials are used throughout their life, an SMM approach seeks to: use materials in the most productive way with an emphasis on using less; reduce toxic chemicals and environmental impacts throughout the material's life cycle; assure we have sufficient resources to meet today's needs and those of the

future." US EPA, *"Sustainable Materials Management Basics,"* epa.gov, n.d., https://www.epa.gov/smm/sustainable-materials-management-basics. Definition of circular economy (see **KEY TERMS** or endnote 2 of **RECYCLED CONTENT**).

2 United States: Paper and paperboard packaging was the major item *sent for recycling* in the United States (representing 67% of all recycling, according to the US EPA). In Canada: paper represented 36% of all materials *diverted* from disposal in Canada in 2018 (Statistics Canada, *Table 38-10-0034-01 Materials diverted, by type, inactive, released February 16, 2021*, https://www150.statcan.gc.ca/n1/en/catalogue/3810003401), followed by organics (29%); construction, renovation, and demolition materials (7%), ferrous metal (6%)%), and tires (4 %). Corrugated boxes sent for recycling in Canada was estimated by the Paper & Paperboard Packaging Environmental Council (PPEC) at 85% in 2019. Ontario's residential Blue Box program has reported a 98% "recovery" rate for used corrugated boxes for the past four years (Stewardship Ontario Blue Box data). (United States): Paper and paperboard packaging was the major item sent for recycling in the US (representing 67% of all recycling, according to the US EPA. *See the entry on* **WASTE** (**DEFINITIONS**).

3 John Mullinder, "Climate Change Demands That Our Focus Should Be On Improving Paper And Organics Recovery, Not Fiddling Around With Plastic Straws," PPEC, May 15, 2019 (Reposted May 15, 2020) https://johnmullinder.ca/climate-change-demands-that-our-focus-should-be-on-improving-paper-and-organics-recovery-not-fiddling-around-with-plastic-straws/.

4 Elizabeth Elkin, "Green Packaging Isn't Good Enough Anymore," *Bloomberg News*, May 8,2021: https://www.bloomberg.ca/green-packaging-isn-t-good-enough-anymore-1.1600964. "China banned free plastic bags at markets in 2008 and made a goal of eliminating non-degradable plastic straw by 2020, but the government has had trouble making markets, restaurants, and the public follow these guidelines. Tang Damin, plastic analyst at Greenpeace East Asia, said part of the problem is how top-down the initiative has been: plastic pollution can't be tackled without consumers wanting to make the effort."

5 John Mullinder, "No Good Box Should Go to the Dump!" April 20, 2015. (Reprinted 2018 in *Packaging and the Environment*, https://johnmullinder.ca/wp-content/uploads/2018/12/Book-of-Blogs_July_27-2.pdf.

6 Change may be coming soon. Some 36 members of the global Consumer Goods Forum have committed to two "Golden Rules" aimed at using less and better plastic to reduce the complexity of plastics recycling and to increase its recycling rates. The first "Rule" focusses on increasing the value of PET bottle recycling by using transparent and uncoloured PET or transparent blue or green in all PET bottles, and ensuring that material choice, adhesive choice, and the size of sleeves or labels are not problematic for recycling. The second "Rule" is to remove problematic elements from packaging (no undetectable carbon black, no PVC or PVDC, no EPS or PS, no PETG in rigid plastic packaging and no oxo-degradable). The members represent more than 10% of the global plastics packaging market and have committed to adopt these rules wherever possible by 2025. Postscript: Several further "Rules" have now been published. Consumer Goods Forum, "CGF Plastic Waste Coalition Launches Full Set of 'Golden Design Rules' to

Tackle Plastic Waste" (press release), the consumergoodsforum.com, July 13, 2021, www.theconsumergoodsforum.com/press_releases/cgf-plastic-waste-coalition-launches-full-set-of-golden-design-rules-to-tackle-plastic-waste/ and "Golden Design Rules: For Optimal Plastic Design, Production and Recycling" (full details), the consumergoodsforum.com, July 13, 2021, https://www.theconsumergoodsforum.com/wp-content/uploads/2021/07/2021-Plastics-All-Golden-Design-Rules-One-Pager.pdf.

7 Stewardship Ontario Blue Box data for the years 2003 through 2019. See also John Mullinder, "Blue Box Recycling: Who's Performing and Who's Not," PPEC, January 28, 2020, https://ppec-paper.com/blue-box-recycling-whos-performing-and-whos-not/.

8 Stewardship Ontario, ibid., 2019, *Table 1: Generation and Recovery and Table 2: Gross and Net Costs.*

RESPONSIBLE SOURCING (CHAIN-OF-CUSTODY CERTIFICATION)

1 Environmental groups brand competing forest certifying agencies as "industry-run." But the FSC has come under fire too. See Richard Conniff, "Greenwashed Timber: How Sustainable Forest Certification Has Failed," *Yale Environment 360*, 20, (online), February 20, 2018. https://e360.yale.edu/features/greenwashed-timber-how-sustainable-forest-certification-has-failed.

2 Consumer Goods Forum, https://www.consumergoodsforum.com

REUSABLE

1 The former Canadian Plastics Industry Association (All About Bags) website quoted a study involving a girls' soccer team playing in Washington State. The team became infected with Norovirus, which scientists later determined came from a reusable grocery bag. Tests revealed that the virus was on the sides of the bag below the handle, Lucy Campbell, "Reusable Shopping Bags Contaminated with Deadly Bacteria." lawyersandsettlements.com, May 16, 2012, https://www.lawyersandsettlements.com/lawsuit/reusable-shopping-bags-contaminated-with-deadly.html. The website mentioned two studies, one in the United States and one in Canada, that showed bacterial loading of the bags increased with repeated use, and that such bags could be a breeding ground for bacteria and other coliforms.

2 Corrugated Packaging Alliance ,"LCA Shows Balanced Environmental Results for Produce Container Systems," (press release,), June 19, 2019. https://www.corrugated.org/lca-shows-balanced-environmental-results-for-produce-container-systems/. The full Corrugated Life Cycle Assessment (LCA) is available for download here: https://www.corrugated.org/corrugated-life-cycle-assessment/.

3 Siyun Wang, Keith Warriner *et al.*, "Microbiological Status of Reusable Plastic Containers in Commercial Grower/Packer Operations and Risk of *Salmonella* Cross-Contamination Between Containers and Cucumbers," *Food Control*, volume 110, 107021, April 2020, https://sciencedirect.com/science/article/abs/pii/S0956713519306103?dgcid=autho. See also John Mullinder, "Salmonella Survives Plastic Crate Washing Test, Transfers to Fresh Cucumber," PPEC, December 4, 2019 https://johnmullinder.ca/

salmonella-survives -plastic -crate -washing -test, -transfers -to -fresh -cucumber, John Mullinder, December 4, 2019./. By comparison, in a typical paper mill recycling process, the temperature of the paper sheet reaches 220 to 240 degrees Fahrenheit, well above 100 degrees Celsius, the boiling point of water and the temperature required for sterilization. The converting process (board into box) also involves high temperatures and other hygiene controls. Having a fresh box every time minimizes the potential for undesirable pathogens and bacteria being carried forward to the consumer. A recent independent study of corrugated produce boxes showed that the corrugation process destroys bacteria. (Haley & Aldrich, Inc., November 19, 2015 (letter), https://www.ccca-box.org/wp-content/uploads/2017/04/Final-HA-CorrugatedHeatStudy_2015_1119.pdf).

SUGARCANE (BAGASSE)

1   Author correspondence with Bob Hurter, President of Hurter Consult, past chair of Nonwood Fibers Committee, Technical Association of Pulp and Paper Industry (TAPPI).

2   . "Acid-free paper," Wikipedia, https://en.wikipedia.org/wiki/Acid-free-paper, accessed October 14, 2021.

3   Ledesma in Argentina https://ledesma.com/

4   Stop Sugarcane Burning website of the Sierra Club Florida http://stopsugarburning.org/the-burning-problem/#gallery

5   An analysis of the Sugar Sheet Paper by Trucost in March 2017 says the impacts from raw material use were assumed to be reduced for the Sugar Sheet paper "since the key raw material (bagasse) is an agricultural waste product which would otherwise be disposed" (p.11). This is a false assumption, as pointed out above. The environmental impact of coal substitution in the sugar mill's boilers is missing from the analysis as well. An earlier analysis for TreeZero Paper Products (done by Verus Carbon Neutral in 2010) also ignores the fact that bagasse is the fuel for the sugar mill boilers (and why it is incinerated). In Colombia, the replacement fuel for bagasse would be coal. There is also no mention of the carbon dioxide (and particulate) emissions, or of the ash issues from pre-harvest sugarcane field burning, which is the practice in Colombia.

6   "Earth Friendly Bagasse Sugarcane Bowls Are Perfect for Hot and Cold Food," ecokloud.com, n.d., www.ecokloud.com/biodegradable/compostable/bagasse-bowls.html. Accessed August 9, 2021.

7   Section 8.3: "If a self-declared environmental claim involves a comparison with other products, then a description of the method used, the results of any tests of those products, or any of the assumptions made shall be clearly stated." Section 9: "Comparative claims always require an explanatory statement to identify the benchmark against which they have been evaluated. The comparison shall only be made using a published standard or recognized test method." Section 5.9: "It is not permissible to shift the environmental burden from one stage of a product's life to another and then make a claim concerning the improved stage without considering whether there is in fact a net overall environmental benefit. Environmental claims should be based on the best available information in each life cycle phase of the product to assess the net environmental benefit associated with a

claim." Competition Bureau of Canada, "5.9," "8.3 Access to information," and "9 Comparative Claims," *Environmental Claims: A Guide for Industry and Advertisers*," June 2008, https://www.competitionbureau.gc.ca/eic/site/cb-bc.nsf/eng/02701.html

8   Section 260.2: "In the context of environmental marketing claims, a reasonable basis often requires competent and reliable scientific evidence. Such evidence consists of tests, analyses, research, or studies that have been conducted and evaluated in an objective manner by qualified persons and are generally accepted in the profession to yield accurate and reliable results. Such evidence should be sufficient in quality and quantity based on standards generally accepted in the relevant scientific fields, when considered in the light of the entire body or relevant scientific evidence, to substantiate that each of the marketing claims is true." Section260.4 (b): "... marketers should not make unqualified general environmental benefit claims." US Federal Trade Commission, "260.2 Interpretation and Substantiation of Environmental Marketing Claims," and "260.4(b) General Environmental Benefit Claims," *Green Guides (Revised)*, October 1, 2012, https://www.ftc.gov/sites/default/files/attachments/press-releases/ftc-issues-revised-green-guides/greenguides.pdf.

SUSTAINABLE

1   The US Federal Trade Commission's *Green Guides* states it does not address the use of the term *sustainable* "either because the FTC lacks a sufficient basis to provide meaningful guidance or wants to avoid proposing guidance that duplicates or contradicts rules or guidance of other agencies." (US Federal Trade Commission, "FTC Issues Revised 'Green Guides'" (press release), October 1, 2012, https://www.ftc.gov/news-events/press-releases/2012/10/ftc-issues-revised-green-guides. Canada's Competition Bureau states: "At this time there are no definitive methods for measuring sustainability or confirming its accomplishment. Therefore, no claim of achieving sustainability shall be made." (Competition Bureau of Canada, "4.6. Claims of Sustainability." *Environmental Claims: A Guide for Industry and Advertisers*, June 2008, https://www.competitionbureau.gc.ca/eic/site/cb-bc.nsf/eng/02701.html

2   Canadian Council of Forest Ministers, *Measuring our Progress our Progress: Putting Sustainable Forest Management Into Practice Across Canada and Beyond*, 2020, https://www.ccfm.org/wp-content/uploads/2020/08/Measuring-our-progress-Putting-sustainable-forest-management-into-practice-across-Canada-and-beyond.pdf.

3   Sustainable Forest Management backgrounder at www.nrcan.gc.ca/forests/canada/sustainable-forest-management/13183.

4   Argentina, Australia, Canada, Chile, Japan, Republic of Korea, Mexico, New Zealand, Russian Federation, United States of America, and Uruguay (www.montrealprocess.org).

5   47%, Natural Resources Canada, *The State of Canada's Forests, Annual Report 2019*, p.6, https://d1ied5g1xfgpx8.cloudfront.net/pdfs/40084.pdf.

6   Certification Canada (https://certificationcanada.org/en/home/).

TOILET PAPER

1   Jennifer Skene (with Shelley Vinyard), *The Issue with Tissue*, Natural Resources Defense Council (NRDC) and STAND.earth, February 2019., https://stand.earth/sites/default/files/StandEarth-NRDC-IssueWithTissue-Report.pdf.

2   See "**TREE-FREE**" for comment about the claims being made for wheat straw.

3   Natural Resources Canada, *The State of Canada's Forests, Annual Report, 2020*, 2020, *p.63.*, https://www.nrcan.gc.ca/our-natural-resources/forests-forestry/state-canadas-forests-report/16496. Some 747,690 hectares of Canada's 346,964,664 hectares of forest land were harvested in 2018 (0.21%). That means that 99.8% was not harvested.

4   See **BOREAL FOREST**. The boreal forest is found in seven of Canada's 12 distinct terrestrial ecozones. While the boreal forest makes up a large area of Canada's total forest area (82%), it accounts for only three-fifths of the area harvested, according to a Canadian Forest Service analysis covering the years 2000 to 2015. The numbers are 453,600 hectares harvested from between 270 and 285 million hectares of boreal forest (there's a variation because of different mapping interpretations). That's 0.15% or 0.16%.

5   The harvest is mostly for lumber to build houses, hospitals, schools, and so on. What's left over (wood chips, shavings, and sawdust) is certainly used for other purposes (to supply energy to a mill and to the local community, and to make paper products) but the prime purpose of that harvest is for the lumber, not paper products. That's why when people are not building houses (for example, in a recession) that overall harvest numbers go way down. (The harvest on provincial land in the recession year of 2009 was the lowest since 1990). Calculating the portion of boreal harvest that goes specifically to make toilet paper is rather tricky because the sawmill residues that are used are later converted to paper both inside and outside Canada, and into other products as well (printing and writing paper, towelling, and even some packaging grades). However, assuming that other countries use pulp in a similar way to Canada, the Forest Products Association of Canada (FPAC) estimates that less than 5% of Canadian-produced wood pulp, and less than 1% of total harvested wood (not just from the boreal), ends up in toilet paper each year. (Also note that about 60% of toilet paper in Canada comes from recycled paper).

6   One-quarter of Canada's certified forests are certified to FSC. NRDC calls FSC's forest certification program robust, respected, offering "superior sustainability," the strongest certification in Canada. See also John Mullinder, "US Group Telling Canada How to Manage Its Forests," johnmullinder.ca, May 14, 2021, https://johnmullinder.ca/us-group-telling-canada-how-to-manage-its-forests/

7   *The Issue with Tissue*, ibid., p.13. See the entry on **HYPOCRISY?** Todd Paglia, executive director of ForestEthics quoted in "FPAC Commits to New Forest Management Approach to Mimic Elements of Nature," (press release for Forest Products Association of Canada,), Fastmarket's RISI Technology Channels (online), January 14, 2016., https://technology.risiinfo.com/mills/north-america/fpac-commits-new-forest-management-approach-mimic-elements-nature. Other participating environmental organizations included Canadian Parks and Wilderness Society, Ivey Foundation, The Nature Conservancy, TNC Canada, International Boreal Conservation Campaign, and the Schad Foundation.

8   See **RECYCLED CONTENT** for a discussion on the false arguments being used to promote post-consumer recycled content.

9   See **"ANCIENT" FORESTS** and **"OLD-GROWTH" FOREST.** The great majority of Canada's forests are relatively young, aged between 41 and 120 years old, with most of them in the 81 to 100-year range. Not exactly *centuries old!* As for the boreal, only 1% of its trees is more than 200 years old. Yes, 1% (National Forest Inventory [Canada} database).

"TREE-FREE"

1   Robert C. Williams Museum of Papermaking, Georgia Tech, Renewable Bioproducts Institute.

2   John Mullinder, "Newsprint Excellence: A History of Technical Innovation in the Canadian Newsprint Industry," supplement in *Pulp & Paper Journal*, 1989, Maclean Hunter Ltd.

3   "Tree-Free Paper: A Path to Saving Trees and Forests?" twosidesna.org July 18, 2014, https://twosidesna.org/US/tree-free-paper-a-path-to-saving-trees-and-forests/; and Dr. Jim Bowyer *et al.*, "Tree-Free Paper: A Path to Saving Trees and Forests," Dovetail Partners, released July 9, 2014, revised August 19, 2014, https://www.dovetailinc.org/report pdfs/2014/dovetailtreefree0714.pdf

4   Michael D'Estries, Woody Harrelson Hoping Tree-Free Paper Takes Off," Mother Nature Network, June 15, 2010. www.mnn.com/lifestyle/arts-culture/blogs/woody-harrelson-hoping-tree-free-paper-takes-off

5   Melissa Breyer, "Woody Harrelson Fights for the Forests with his Tree-Free Paper Company", Mother Nature Network, June 25, 2013. https://www.mnn.com/money/sustainable-business-practices/stories/woody-harrelson-fights-for-the-forests-with-his-tree

6   Valerie Langer, "Modern Pulp Mill Using Agricultural Fibers, Not Trees, Starts Construction in US," Canopy, November 14, 2017. http://canopyplanet.org/groundbreaking-news-literally/

7   *SURVIVAL: A Plan for Saving Forests and Climate, A Pulp Thriller*, 2020, Canopy www.canopyplanet.org/wp-content/uploads/2020/01/SURVIVAL-Next-Gen-Pathway.pdf.

8   "Packaging Zeitgeist Expands to World's Endangered Forests and Climate," (media release) Canopy, October 1, 2019 https://canopyplanet.org/packaging-zeitgeist-expands-to-worlds-endangered-forests-and-climate/

9   John Mullinder, "Brand Owners Sucked in by Canopy's Embarrassing Boo-Boos," PPEC, October 17, 2019 (Reposted johnmullinder.ca, October 23, 2019, https://johnmullinder.ca/brand-owners-sucked-in-by-canopys-embarrassing-boo-boos/; "Canopy Makes More Embarrassing 'Boo-Boos'", PPEC, March 2, 2020 (Reposted, https://johnmullinder.ca/canopy-makes-more-embarrassing-boo-boos/ and "Canopy's Wheat Straw Dream is Missing a Few Key Facts," johnmullinder.ca, February 16, 2021, https://www.johnmullinder.ca/canopys-wheat-straw-dream-is-missing-a-few-key-facts/

10   Sonja N. Oswalt *et al., Forest Resources of the United States 2017: A Technical Document Supporting the blue Forest Service 2020 RPA Assessment,* (Gen. Tech. Report WO-97), US Department of Agriculture Forest Service. March 2019, https://www.fs.fed.us/research/publications/gtr/gtr_wo97.pdf.

11   Jeffrey. V. Wells*, et al.,* "The State of Conservation in North America's Boreal Forest: Issues and Opportunities," *Frontiers in Forests and Global Change,* July 30, 2020. https://doi.org/10.3389/ffgc.2020.00090 "Using Crowther *et al's* (2015) boreal tree density average applied to the North American Boreal Forest biome that the biome holds as many as 500 billion individual trees."

12   Natural Resources Canada, *The State of Canada's Forests, Annual Report 2020,* (427 million seedlings/year).

13   Valeria Langer, What's in the Box? Part 1, Canopy, November 26, 2019. https://canopyplanet.org/whats-in-the-box-part-1/

14   "Most Canadian Packaging Board Now 100% Recycled Content," (press release), Paper & Paperboard Packaging Environmental Council (PPEC), September 12, 2019, https://www.ppec-paper.com/most-canadian-packaging-board-now-100-recycled-content/.

15   "Pioneering the Recycling of Old Boxboard Cartons", Fact Sheet 31, 2019, Paper & Paperboard Packaging Environmental Council (PPEC), https://www.ppec-paper.com/pdfFiles/factsheets/2019/The3Rs/FS31-2019.pdf

16   Natural Resources Canada, *The State of Canada's Forests, Annual Report 2020,* ibid. Hectares deforested in 2018 were 34,257 hectares of 347,964,664 hectares of forest land (0.0098%). The major causes were mining and oil and gas development (39%) and conversion of forest land to agriculture (36%). Forestry as a whole was responsible for the deforestation of 1,494 hectares of Canada's forest lands (0.0004%) through the creation of new permanent access roads.

17   Pack4Good Campaign "Did You Know," Canopy, n.d. https://canopyplanet.org/campaigns/pack4good/: and Laura Repas, "188 global groups say it's time to 'make the throw-away go away,'" Canopy, February 16, 2021, https://canopyplanet.org/188-global-groups-say-its-time-to-make-the-throw-away-go-away/

18   World Business Council for Sustainable Development, *Facts & Trends: Fresh & Recycled Fiber Complementarity* (2015). https://www.wbcsd.org/Sector-Projects/Forest-Solutions-Group/Resources/Facts-Trends-Fresh-Recycled-Fiber-Complementarity

19   Statistics Canada, *Table 38-10-0034-01 Materials diverted, by type,* inactive, released February 16, 2021. https://www150.statcan.gc.ca/t1/tbl1/en/tv.action?pid=3810003401.

20   John Mullinder, "Blue Box Recycling: Who's Performing and Who's Not," PPEC, January 28, 2020. (Reposted, https://johnmullinder.ca/blue-box-recycling-whos-performing-and-whos-not/.

21   Carl Meyer, "The New Green Paper Sector Doesn't Need Trees," *Toronto Star* (online), February 9, 2021. https://www.thestar.com/news/canada/2021/02/09/the-new-green-paper-sector-doesnt-need-trees.html

22 *Toronto Star*, ibid.

23 SURVIVAL, *A Plan for Saving Forests and Climate*, Canopy, ibid.

24 "Appendix B- Independent Engineer's Report", Columbia Pulp Bond Issue Limited Offering Memorandum dated July 24, 2017.

25 Life Cycle Analysis and Carbon Footprint https://www.columbiapulp.com/wp-content/uploads/2019/11/LCA-Presentation-1-9-19.pdf (accessed August 15, 2021)

26 SURVIVAL, *A Plan for Saving Forests and Climate*, Canopy, ibid.

27 "Estimated Sources and Uses of Funds," Columbia Pulp Bond Issue Limited Offering Memorandum dated July 25, 2019, p. 18.

28 "Appendix C-2-*Market Analysis for Columbia Pulp's Co-Product* (June 28, 2017). "Columbia Pulp Bond Issue Limited Offering Memorandum dated July 24, 2017. Based on Table 5, p. 14.

29 Columbia Pulp Bond Issue Limited Offering Memorandum dated July 24, 2017, p. 10. Projected revenue from sale of co-product for 2023 of $42 million of total revenue $123.3 million (34%).

30 Columbia Pulp website www.columbiapulp.com/our-products/bio-polymer/ (accessed June 4, 2021) identifies four possible markets for this black liquor. One of them, using it for dust control on roads, got Domtar into trouble with Ontario's Ministry of Environment years ago because of fears of environmental damage through run-off. Another, using it as a fertilizer performance enhancer, may encounter trouble too. Columbia Pulp's black liquor is sodium-based. Land application and crop production are sensitive to any source of sodium. See these two studies: "Diagnosis and Improvements of Saline and Alkali Soils" (Agricultural Handbook No. 60, 1954) and "Agricultural Salinity and Drainage" (Hanson *et al*, 1996). There is also an online FAO textbook by R.S. Ayers and D.W. Westcott, *Water Quality for Agriculture*, fao.org (reprinted 1989, 1994), https://www.fao.org/fileadmin/user_upload/kagera/resource/NRL_SLMcatalogue_2013.pdf Section 3.1f (Water quality for agriculture) outlines the negative effects of high sodium.

WASTE (DEFINITIONS)

1 "Canadians are "among the world's champion garbage creators.", Bob Weber/*The Canadian Press*, "Canadians Creating More Waste and Lack Solutions: Report," citynews.ca, March 9, 2018., https://www.toronto.citynews.ca/2018/03/09/canadians-waste/

2 OECD oecd.org/about/

3 Silpa Kaza *et al*., *What a Waste 2.0: A Global Snapshot of Solid Waste Management to 2050*. Urban Development, Washington DC., World Bank. © World Bank, 2018, https://openknowledge.worldbank.org/handle/10986/30317. See also Hristina Byrnes and Thomas C. Frohlich "Canada Produces the Most Waste in the World. The US Ranks Third," *24/7 Wall Street* (*USA Today* online), July 12, 2019., https://www.usatoday.com/story/money/2019/07/12/canada-united-states-worlds-biggest-producers-of-waste/39534923/.

The top 10 waste producers in this study were Canada (36.1 metric tonnes per capita), Bulgaria, the United States (25.9 metric tonnes per capita), Estonia, Finland, Armenia, Sweden, Luxembourg, Ukraine, and Serbia.

4   To convert metric tonnes to short tons, multiply by 1.102. To convert short tons to metric tonnes, divide by 1.102.

5   Residential and non-residential splits were not provided at the total level in 2018 because electronic and tire source data was unavailable. The splits shown here are therefore calculated from the splits for 94% of total material diversion (electronics and tires representing the remaining 6%).

XMAS PAPER

1   Olivia Bowden, "We Toss 540K Tonnes of Wrapping Paper After the Holidays – Here's How to Give Without the Garbage," *Global News*, (online), November 29, 2019. https://globalnews.ca/news/6229467/we-toss-540k-tonnes-of-wrapping-paper-after-the-holidays-heres-how-to-give-without-the-garbage/. Stephanie Levitz/The Canadian Press, "Canadians Will Throw out 540,000 Tonnes of Wrapping Paper and Gift Bags This Christmas Season," *Toronto Star* (online), December 28, 2017. https://www.thestar.com/news/canada/2017/12/28/canadians-will-throw-out-540000-tonnesof-wrapping-paper-and-gift-bags-this-christmas-season.html. Helena Hanson, "Canadians Throw Away the Weight Of 100,000 Elephants in Wrapping Paper Every Christmas," narcity.com, November 29, 2019. https://www.narcity.com/alternative-gift-wrap-ideas-could-save-540k-tonnes-of-paper-from-landfill. Cat Divaris, "Canadians Throw Away 540,000 Tonnes of Wrapping Paper Every Christmas," Rock95.com, December 2, 2019, https://rock95.com/canadians-throw-away-540000-tonnes-of-wrapping-paper-every-christmas/. Susan Krashinsky-Robertson, "Consumer Backlash Over Plastic Packages Has Retailers Looking for Solutions, But None are Easy," *Globe and Mail*, December 13, 2019, updated December 16, 2019, https://www.theglobeandmail.com/business/article-when-it-comes-to-paper-or-plastic-bags-what-feels-good-for-customers/.

2   "The Holidays Are No Time to Waste," (media release) Recycling Council of British Columbia, December 5, 2007, https://www.rcbc.ca/files/u3/med_xmaswaste2007.pdf.

3   Author email, Mairi Welman, May 19, 2020.

4   *Zero/Waste* 1 No.3 (Winter 2002), Regional District of Nanaimo. Author emails to Meghan Ebueza, March 17-18, 2020.

ZERO WASTE

1   For an excellent article on the debate about net-zero emissions read James Murray "Net Zero Faces Fierce Criticism", greenbiz.com May 10, 2021. https://www.greenbiz.com/article/net-zero-faces-fierce-criticism; first published as "In Defense of Net Zero," businessgreen.com April 30, 2021 https://www.businessgreen.com/blog-post/4030376/defense-net-zero

2 *New Plastics Economy*, Ellen MacArthur Foundation (EMF). Mentioned in *"Definitions for the Circular Economy in Canada"*, Dan Lantz. Interestingly, the EMF doesn't speak to the sustainable materials management approach where reduction of resource consumption up front is the first priority.

3 Zero Waste International Alliance, quoted in "Definitions for the Circular Economy in Canada," ibid.

4 Zero Waste Europe, quoted in "Definitions for the Circular Economy in Canada," ibid.

5 Canadian Council of Ministers for the Environment (CCME), *Canada-Wide Action Plan on Zero Plastic Waste, Phase 1*, (PN 1589) June 27, 2019, p.3, https://ccme.ca/en/res/1589_ccmecanada-wideactionplanonzeroplasticwaste_en-secured.pdf

Manufactured by Amazon.ca
Bolton, ON

25671410R00109